THE PEOPLE'S
MADONNA

By the same author,
available from HarperCollins

MOTHER OF NATIONS

THE PEOPLE'S MADONNA

by
Joan Ashton

Foreword by
Robert Llewelyn

Fount
An Imprint of HarperCollins*Publishers*

First published in Great Britain
in 1991 by Fount Paperbacks

Fount Paperbacks is an imprint of
HarperCollinsReligious
Part of HarperCollinsPublishers
77–85 Fulham Palace Road, London W6 8JB

Typeset by Medcalf Type Ltd, Bicester, Oxon
Printed and bound in Great Britain by
HarperCollins Manufacturing, Glasgow

A catalogue record for this book
is available from the British Library

Contents

Foreword

The remarkable happenings at Medjugorje over the
past ten years have captured the imagination of many
in the western world. More than a million visitors each
year flock into this small isolated village in Yugoslavia
to share in the life of its people, to be uplifted and
refreshed by the worship in its parish church, and to
meet with the visionaries as they distil Mary's
messages to groups gathered in the forecourts of their
houses. I have myself had the privilege of speaking
personally with two of the visionaries – with the
vibrant, friendly, outgoing Vicka, and the serenely
happy, contemplative Marija – and of all these young
people I can bear witness that their openness and
candour, their radiance and joy, speak more eloquently
than any words of the transforming vision they have
received.

Words can, however, take us some of the way, and
Joan Ashton has in these pages shared with us her own
vision of Medjugorje, and invited us to travel, at least
in spirit, to that extraordinary village where, for a
while, normal occupations are put aside, that the heart

may be free to make its journey to its resting place in God. In Medjugorje you do not plan; you open your heart to God (or Jesus or Mary according to your way) and you will be taken to what is right for you: the sermon, the visionary, the fellow-pilgrim, whatever it may be. I have seen this happen to others and experienced it myself in a remarkable way. As likely as not your guide will give you this advice as you travel by coach from the airport to your lodgings in the village.

Joan Ashton, author of *Mother of Nations*, is well qualified for her task, for she has visited and captured the spirit of a number of Marian shrines, as will be already known to those who have read her richly informative book. She has made five visits to Medjugorje, and met with and interviewed many at the heart of its life. She writes as an Anglican Christian deeply committed to the authenticity of the visions. She believes with me that here are six young people who see Mary before them at certain times, hold conversation with her as we do with one another, and even on occasions touch and embrace her. Some readers may rub their eyes at that sentence, and we have – and in the nature of things *can* have – only the visionaries' word for its truth. But they have, over the years, allowed themselves to be subjected to batteries of scientific tests from specialists from many countries, and one and all (though science is incompetent to affirm the Marian vision) can find no credible alternative explanation to that which the visionaries offer. Certainly, as science *can* affirm, they are normal and healthy, they are neither play-acting nor hallucinating, nor are there any traces of pathological disturbance. "It is" says Professor Joyeux, leader of a medical team, "like a state of contemplation and encounter with a person whom they alone can see and hear and touch." And although in his scientific capacity he could not state that Mary was appearing at Medjugorje, he seems barely to conceal his personal view in adding, "If God exists, why should this not be possible?"

Medjugorje is a Catholic village, and Mary's teaching is naturally adjusted to practices which Catholics have found fruitful through the ages. Apart from the Eucharist which in one form or another is shared by all Christians, the rosary is the main instrument for the growth of the spirit. But Mary comes to all Christians, indeed to all people ("It is you, not God," she tells us through the visionaries "who have made the divisions") and it cannot but be right that we should be free to adapt her teaching to our various denominations and customs. Mary insists that she has come to lead us to her Son: the rosary is an admirable instrument for this, and at the same time we share the companionship of Mary herself. But it is not the only way, and what matters is that we meet Jesus who is himself the way, the truth and the life. I have myself, in comparatively recent years, become a regular user of the rosary, and I believe that for those who take the pains to discover it, it may open immense riches to millions beyond the Catholic Church. So I would say to Anglicans and other non-Catholics who visit Medjugorje: do not disdain the treasure of the rosary which perhaps, for the first time, you will be offered there. When you travel abroad you will eat the food the country offers. Take, too, if you can, its spiritual treasure and you will not be disappointed.

I have said little about the captivating book Joan Ashton has offered us. Its pages are quite able to stand up for themselves. To read them thoughtfully and reflectively is in itself to make a pilgrimage, and it will surely be that some, when they have finished the course, will want to make the journey to Medjugorje itself. Yet neither the author nor myself would claim that Medjugorje is for all, though we would claim that all Christians should be prayerfully aware (at least it is likely to be a powerful ally in this decade of evangelism) of the explosion of spirituality in that place and its implications for the renewal of society today. History has repeatedly shown – and Jesus draws attention to this (Matthew 23:29–31) – that the Church is likely to honour its prophets only after their day has passed. Will it be so with Mary whose prophetic role is underlined by her first appearance on St John the Baptist Day, and who, like John, comes to point us to Jesus as Lord? Jesus also warned that the childlike in heart – and Mary usually comes to children – will be more spiritually receptive, and so more likely to recognize God's messengers, than those who walk in the wisdom of the world (Matthew 11:25). Therein lies a thought for the searching of hearts, not least, perhaps, within the branches of the Church. It is that we may be helped to understand these things that the author has, at least in part, offered us this book.

Robert Llewelyn

Acknowledgements

I acknowledge with much gratitude the unstinting help given to me by so many people in the course of writing this book. I particularly want to thank Giles Semper and Robert Llewelyn for encouraging me to begin and to go on, and the English-speaking Friars in Medjugorje – Fathers Slavko Barberic, Philip Pavic and Svetozar Kraljevic – who gave me so generously of their time, besides Fathers George Tüttö and Jim Nicholls who made these talks possible. The patient help of Prebendary John Pearce in reading and commenting on the draft chapters was inestimable, and my great thanks also go to Joy Alexander, who not only checked the whole manuscript but also typed it.

All scriptural quotations are from the Jerusalem Bible, Popular edition, published by Darton, Longman and Todd 1968, and are used by kind permission.

Introduction:
Slavko Investigates

A unique and most extraordinary event is currently taking place, though still unknown to the great majority of people. This is the alleged appearance daily since 24 June 1981 of the Virgin Mary at Medjugorje[1] in Yugoslavia.

Claims of such appearances have been made many times before, but a tendency to dismiss them as something intended for and understood by the Roman Catholic Church only is to miss the point, since what these still existing daily visits could be about is a rescue operation on the grandest, most international and most non-denominational scale since the time of Christ. Father Slavko has found that it is an event corroborated moreover by the evidence of people who were neither Roman Catholics nor believers.

Slavko Barberic was born in a place called Dragicina, only a few miles from Medjugorje, in the year that peace succeeded six years of world war (1945) and grew

1 Pronounced Med you gory a. As a rough guide to the pronunciation of names etc. j becomes y, and c becomes ch.

up in a part of the country whose priests had for centuries been friars. He chose to become a Franciscan friar himself, and was ordained in 1971. He completed his studies, serving as a priest for a year in Graz, Austria and five years in Capljina, Yugoslavia before writing a doctoral thesis at Freiburg university, Germany from 1978–81, by which time he was in touch with the news from Medjugorje that six children there claimed to see the Virgin Mary.

He asked the permission of his Superior to go and investigate.

When he arrived in Medjugorje in January 1982 the alleged daily visions had been taking place for the past six months.

His approach was perhaps that of an optimistic sceptic influenced by two considerations: his recently acquired doctorate in religious education, conversion and psychotherapy and the fact that he was a local lad. He was therefore well qualified to make an objective study at first hand of what was happening by putting his doctorate to the test; and he understood the culture, background, psychology and possible motives of the children involved.

Although his immediate intuition on arrival was that they were telling the truth he was at the same time disappointed, since he had concluded while at Freiburg that he would find a simple case of fantasy and collusion. Yet none of the children tried to convince him, as he had expected, and all of them were reluctant to say more than ''Yes, we see the Madonna''. Why did they not try to convince him?

By a dispassionate and careful step-by-step analysis,

he considered various hypotheses and ascertained which factors were not present. The children were not hallucinating nor lying; they were neither alcoholics nor of unsound mind; telekinesis was not involved; if they were being hypnotized, who and where was the hypnotist? And if the joy and peace they experienced was drug-induced, why was such a drug unknown?

On the positive side, while the children formed a group, their characters and interests were disparate; they were not close friends, and they had no leader such as do normal peer groups who are organized for a common interest, for example sport or study. As a group they transcended all normal rules. They stayed together for the visions only; and they were *never afraid*, either of what had happened or of what might happen, though consoling the fears of others.

The only possible leader or organizer was Father Jozo Zovko, who was with them for the first six weeks before being imprisoned by the Communist authorities; yet after his arrest the group went on as before. If there is no shared interest a group customarily ceases; how then did this one carry on and who organized it?

Between 9 January and 24 June 1982, the date of the first anniversary of the visions, he spoke for thirty evenings to each child separately, but never in the same order, so that they had no means of preparing or comparing what they said. It became clear that they spoke of what they were seeing, and that it seemed to them an obvious state of affairs, about which they had already been questioned relentlessly.

All continued to insist to Slavko ''We see her'', and

that she spoke to them of peace and prayer. *Could* it, then, be the Madonna?

He concluded reluctantly that his initial intuition had been correct, and he felt obliged to accept what they said until it was disproved. They were all healthy and ordinary; were they also, like St Paul[2], instruments of God?

Slavko's knowledge of six languages enables him to communicate with the pilgrims, said to have exceeded twelve million by the end of 1989, who have come to Medjugorje from almost every country in the world; and he is in no doubt that what is occurring there concerns all Christians and indeed all humanity, and not merely Roman Catholics like himself. Because he represents the country, the place and the people and his personality and qualifications are those required for a continuing and objective appraisal; and because he has contrived to remain there since his arrival in January 1982 apart from several European lecture tours and despite many local difficulties, he has probably come to be regarded as an ambassador for the message of Medjugorje.

Asked of the future, he says that he is no prophet, knowing and doing only what God asks of him from one day to the next; and that when the visions cease, so may the Medjugorje pilgrimages.

Medjugorje's history symbolizes war, racial conflict, religious persecution, envy and murder. By his heritage, education and vocation, Slavko is well equipped to point to the path of peace, believing the visions to be about the healing of all hurt and division.

2 Acts of the Apostles 9:15.

FACT OR FICTION?

1
The Rumour

Is this, the age of instant and verifiable news, a time specifically chosen for an unlikely yet crucial phenomenon to occur – if indeed it has occurred?

The ascertainable facts are that on and after Wednesday 24 June 1981 – a significant date in the Christian calendar – in an obscure and mountainous region of Croatia, Hercegovina, in Communist-controlled Yugoslavia, eight mostly teenage children say that they were startled by a very bright light seen suddenly at dusk on a stony hillside near their homes.

The 24th June has for two thousand years or so been celebrated as the birthday of John the Baptist, the man sent by God to warn of Christ's coming and later to identify him: he was "a witness to speak for the light, so that everyone might believe through him".[1]

At the centre of the light was the figure of a woman with, in her arms, an infant which she alternately concealed and revealed, at the same time beckoning

1 St John 1:7.

the dazed children to approach. But they ran away from her, panic-stricken.

This woman, standing in light above the ground, was to appear almost daily for the ensuing ten or more years at the same time of about 6.30 p.m. On the third day, in response to a question from a girl of fifteen named Ivanka, (the first one who saw and who dared to speak) the figure disclosed, "I am the Blessed Virgin Mary."

In 1987 an American Franciscan friar of Yugoslavian descent named Philip Pavic (Pavich), whose parents were born in Croatia, reached Medjugorje. He had asked to be sent there from Israel where he had spent eleven years in the Holy Land as an assistant of pilgrims to the holy places.

When he first heard the news of Medjugorje he was living by the Sea of Galilee and responsible for the church of St Peter on the lake shore. This may have been the place where St Peter the fisherman jumped out of his boat, having recognized Christ (for the third time after his resurrection from death) waiting on the shore; where Christ said, "Come and have breakfast" of bread and the fish he was cooking over a charcoal fire; and where he said to Peter three times, "Feed my sheep".[2]

On the roof of this small church overlooking the beauty of the Sea of Galilee, Father Philip used to pray, asking Christ the pastor and shepherd why there were no longer crowds following him about the lake, and where all the sheep had gone? It then came

2 St John 21:4–17.

to him that the sheep might be going to Medjugorje. Then he thought of John the Baptist, on whose birthday he had been ordained; that John the Baptist was recorded in all four gospels as the Revealer of Christ; and that it was on that date that the vision had first appeared in Medjugorje, revealing an infant to children who were unprejudiced, ignorant of scripture and who could never, he concluded, invent such a tale on such a day.

With a few exceptions these daily appearances in the presence of increasingly large crowds were seen by six people only;

a boy of ten called Jakov (Yackov)
a girl of seventeen, Vicka (Vishka)
a girl of fifteen, Ivanka (Ee *van* Ka)
two girls of sixteen, Mirjana (Miryana) and Marija (Maria)
a boy of sixteen, Ivan (Ee*van*)[3]

The six were average children; ordinary, unrelated and not very close friends who, as far as can be understood, just happened to be about at the time in question: all were born in Bijakovici, (Be yack o vitchy) the village lying at the foot of the hill where the beckoning woman was first seen, though not all were living there when this happened. Two other people – a man of twenty and a girl of thirteen – clearly remember seeing the apparition, but on the first day only. All were engaged in very normal pursuits: two

3 For full names see index.

girls out for a stroll, two boys picking apples, a boy and a girl at home, another girl fetching sheep from the hill.

The children had no difficulty in accepting that the woman seen in light on the hill was indeed the Virgin Mary, saying that they saw and spoke to her as to any other person and that they could touch her, describing her looks as beautiful beyond those of any woman they had ever seen; her eyes blue, her hair dark, her voice musical and gentle, her manner motherly and loving. She wore a white mantle and veil over a grey dress, and round her head were twelve golden stars. They were surprised to find that no one else could see and speak to her.

Alphonse Ratisbonne (chapter 19) made an equally calm assertion after his vision of Mary on 20 January 1842 in Rome, saying, ''I have seen her as I see you''; and the boy Ivan, replying to a question in November 1989, said that he found it a good deal easier to converse with the Virgin daily than with the pilgrims who daily interrogated him about her.

On the second day, Ivanka's first words to Mary were to ask about her mother, who had died alone in hospital a few weeks before 24 June. The Virgin said that her mother was well, happy and near her, with a message for Ivanka that she should obey and care for her grandmother, then too old to work: Ivanka received this information with great emotion. The people sensed that heaven had been attained by one of themselves who was not a particularly devout Catholic, and no more than a good and loving wife and mother while on earth. Perhaps, too, even the communion of saints was an attainable reality, if a woman who had died in April was close to St Mary the Virgin in June.

Against this must be set the view that Ivanka's grief for the loss of her mother had rendered her highly emotional, and hence she was the first to claim that she saw the Mother of God, a likely hallucination induced by her Catholic upbringing and by self-hypnosis.

Also on the second day, the children responded to the beckoning figure, further from the road than before, by running uphill with extraordinary and inexplicable speed and ease over the steep, rocky and thorny distance. When they reached her, they knelt down; one barefoot and all with neither bruise nor scratch. Their flight was observed by the bystanders.

The bright light which was said by the children always to precede and surround the vision was also visible to others, both on the hill and the plain; on the third day many saw the whole village and surrounding area illuminated by three brilliant flashes before the Six again stopped to kneel on the hillside. On another occasion light followed the vision's disappearance, always signalled by a cry from the children of "*Ode!*" – "She's gone!"

Yet the excitement also evoked considerable hesitation in the children as to what it might all mean. The vision's smiling silence was her only response when Mirjana said that the people would not believe their story and would accuse them of being crazy. The noise and confusion of those first days on the hill is recorded on cassette. The crowd are heard asking for descriptions of the apparition, while the children's voices transmit the people's pleas to *Gospa* (the Mother of God or Blessed Virgin Mary) for hope for their deceased and healing for their sick families.

A man named Marinko Ivankovich, working as a motor mechanic in the neighbouring town, gave staunch support and help to the children, fending off the milling crowds and consoling the tearful Ivanka after she had heard of her mother ("you should be laughing, not crying"). He and his wife lived next door to Ivanka and both were convinced from the start that these children, no better or worse than any others, were telling the truth. He said that they were good girls who helped his wife with the washing-up and stayed to watch the colour television: and that "God just picked them up".

When he had grasped what seemed to be happening he went to look for a priest in the rectory, where he got a distinctly cool reception and no promise of spiritual consolation for the troubled Six. So the next day, to be on the safe side, he met them with a supply of holy water which Vicka then cast at the apparition, saying, "If you are really the Madonna, stay with us; if not, please go away." Her grandmother had told her that the devil fears holy water and the practice has been used by Christians since the fourth century. The vision stayed, smiling.

When asked about this incident later, Vicka explained that it is the custom in Bijakovici to bless the houses by sprinkling holy water inside and out, a supply being kept in all Christian families; and that her mother made it by putting blessed salt in water

and then reciting the Creed − "I believe in God etc.";
the prayer of faith to oust the incantation of witchcraft.

Marinko's support and interest led him to keep
careful notes of what was going on in the early stages,
notes which may be of value in the final assessment.
The first records kept by the clergy were confiscated
by the police, who became suspicious of possible
insurrection against the Communist government by
the crowds continually assembling on the hill. Cross-
examination by the police on day four failed to elicit
from the children any denial or contradiction of what
they had already claimed was happening.

Meanwhile, after the holy water episode and
prompted by Marinko, Ivanka asked the vision why
she had come and what it was she wanted, to be told,
"Because there are many believers here. I want to
be with you to convert and reconcile everyone." When
the Six were returning from the hill, exhausted by
the heat and by the press of people, Marija felt
compelled to leave the path. She was seen to kneel
suddenly, exclaiming "The *Gospa*!" (in English, the
Mother of God). She afterwards said that the Virgin
came to her, weeping and bearing a cross of all colours
but without the body of Christ, saying through her
tears, "Peace, Peace, Peace. Be reconciled with God
and each other." Marija found this a profoundly
moving experience.

Other significant events during the first week
included further police action. The children, who had
already been medically examined in the nearest town
of Citluk, were taken to a hospital in the city of Mostar,
there to be seen by a psychiatrist. They were

intimidated by being questioned in a mortuary, told that they had imagined it all, left with psychopaths, and accused of being drug-addicts. Mirjana was particularly distressed by this last accusation and by the suggestion that she was also an epileptic. She lived in Sarajevo with her parents and was only spending the summer in Bijakovici to be with her grandmother; but the final diagnosis was that all six children were physically and mentally healthy. Somewhat shaken by this experience, they returned home and made for the hill, where the Virgin appeared again shortly after six o'clock as usual.

Among those present that evening for the first time was Tomislav Vlasic, one of the Franciscan friars who became the children's helper and never doubted the truth of what they said was happening. He was to suffer a good deal for this unshakeable conviction, and will reappear later in the story.

On the following day the police had a new ploy. Two women social workers were sent to fetch the children for a sightseeing tour, which was prolonged beyond the time of the evening vision with the object of preventing it happening. At the due time they were near a place called Cerno in sight of the Bijakovici hill, when the five children – Ivan was missing – insisted on the car being stopped. They got out, knelt by the roadside and began the Lord's Prayer, looking at the people assembled on the distant hill which was by then brightly lit. The light then moved towards them, a light also seen by the two now thoroughly alarmed social workers, and from this light the Virgin appeared and spoke to the children, though only the light was visible to the two women. When the party reached Medjugorje they went straight to Father Jozo Zovko in the rectory, with whom their conversation was tape-recorded, Jozo regarding the stunned government employees as more eloquent witnesses than the children themselves.

Jozo, parish priest in Medjugorje since the previous November, was away when the visions began, and on his return on 27 June he was not convinced by the wild rumours which were circulating.

On 2 July when he was alone in the church, asking for guidance and praying through the reading about Moses crossing the Red Sea, he heard a clear masculine voice saying, ''Go outside now and protect the children.'' The church was still empty as he made his way to the door, where the children rushed towards him from the left side, crying out, ''Help us, the police are after us.'' There was just time to lock them in an empty room in the rectory before telling a running policeman that ''Yes, he had seen the children.'' The man then ran on.

His doubts over, Jozo returned to the church to thank God, then unaware of an additional blessing: the police had forbidden outdoor gatherings, thus causing people to flock instead to the church, there being no law to prevent them. That evening, with the church filled to capacity, Jozo preached about a loving God who had brought the children of Israel safely through the Red Sea from slavery in Egypt, and sustained them with signs of his presence for forty years in the desert: of Mary's obedience to God's call; and of Mary, Joseph and the Child escaping into Egypt from Herod's massacre of the innocents – the Mary who was with them all that very day.[4]

His sermon was heard by an alert informer, who interpreted it as criticism of the government and incitement to rebellion, since forty years was then the exact duration of Marshal Tito's Communist rule (chapter 11). Jozo refused to retract what he had said, and was arrested and imprisoned, but not before he had himself seen Mary. His faith was not extinguished by eighteen months' imprisonment, during which time she came to him again.

Jozo was not alone in sustaining persecution with equanimity; when the children asked if they would be able to bear the strain of continual harassment and interrogation, they were comforted by hearing the *Gospa* say, ''You will endure it, my Angels.''

4 Exodus chapters 14 and 16. Matthew 2:13.

2
For Everyone

Antipathy is hardly too strong a word to define the mutual distrust and suspicion aroused in the minds and hearts of people of differing backgrounds or denominations where acknowledgement of the role of the Virgin Mary is concerned.

This may be partly due to an Anglican inability to shake off the folk-memory of sixteenth-century Mariolatry, and a tendency to look askance at what they regard as the Roman Catholic cult of "Our Lady", pilgrimages to places where she is said to have appeared being looked upon as the ultimate folly; and partly because Catholics tend to be deeply shocked by the merely rather cool deference with which most Anglicans acknowledge St Mary the Virgin.

There is a not unreasonable belief that Roman Catholics are the only people likely to be drawn to Medjugorje, and that others cannot be expected to understand or take part in what is happening there; so the discovery that this Yugoslavian village increasingly attracts those of every shade of belief and of none comes as a surprise to many people.

Robert Faricy, once a sailor now a Jesuit priest, went to Medjugorje for the first time in 1981 and is convinced that the Mother of God appears there as the Mother of all humanity foretold by Christ (St John 19:27). For him the central meaning of Medjugorje is that the events there are for everyone, and will have a different but special meaning for each one. A Nonconformist who was there one Christmas understood the need for tolerance, and the twin pitfalls of Mary-worship and the failure to recognize her; while a Church of England mother, having always accepted Mary intellectually, was persuaded to join a Roman Catholic pilgrimage. She was surprised by her welcome and astonished to feel that Mary *was* her Mother, and that she had a responsibility to tell others of this, though her relationship with her own mother was loving.

More will be said of what the Six claim are the spoken messages they have received from the Virgin; but on 29 June, six days after it all began and when asked by the children what she expected of the assembled crowd, her reported words were

There is only one God, one faith. Let the people believe firmly and do not fear anything. In God there are no religions, there are no divisions, but you men have made divisions.

These words trouble some theologians, since they suggest the indifferentism which makes no distinction between Christ and the prophet Mohammed. "All are equal before God" is Vicka's understanding of the message. But historically the reported words have a particular relevance to peace in Hercegovina. There these man-made divisions are symbolized by the distribution of religious adherence, where one third of the people are Eastern Orthodox, one third Roman Catholics and one third Moslem; in Yugoslavia as a whole there are almost twice as many Orthodox as Roman Catholic Christians, the Moslems numbering less than half the Catholics. In Hercegovina the representatives of these three faiths are in conflict with each other, and have been so for four hundred years. The call, well understood by the six visionary Catholics, must be to every person, and is paraphrased by the French Abbé Laurentin, possibly the greatest authority on worldwide alleged appearances of the Virgin Mary, as "love your brothers, the Orthodox Serbians, the Croatian Moslems and the atheist Marxists who govern you". It is an ecumenism of love, national and religious confusion being local only. For Vicka the universal significance of the message is clear: all people, equal before God, must be respected whatever their religion.

Medjugorje is increasingly visited by Orthodox Christians from Serbia, as well as by Moslems. A Moslem woman named Pasa Djano was with Mirjana in Sarajevo during a vision, and saw a light; but later during an illness she also saw Mary, who confirmed to Mirjana the truth of this report, telling her that the piety of this woman was a model for everyone.

The belief in the West that Mary appears only to Roman Catholics is, however, well-founded, since all the great Marian shrines throughout the world, with the exception of Walsingham in England where responsibility is shared, are in the care of the Roman Catholic Church. That Church's reverence for the Virgin may be the reason why Mary so often makes herself visible to Roman Catholics and so seldom to those other Christians who may hold a sceptical or suspicious view of her alleged appearances, and who perhaps fail to grasp that the Virgin Mary is about the Christian message and not about herself: that she brought God to us and does so still; and that as in Eastern Orthodox icons or pictures, she is always pointing away from herself and towards her Child.

There are reliable reports of Mary's appearance to non-Catholics, including that of an Englishman on Podbrdo Hill, site of the first visions, who saw in white light the silhouette of a woman with her hands, in golden light, spread in blessing. As he gazed the interpreter repeated the visionaries' description of the same figure. He remained cool and detached, though in no doubt of what he had seen, and was granted the corroboration of three more visions of Mary before leaving Medjugorje. It should perhaps be added that for some twenty years the man in question has been gifted with seeing the aura or energy field surrounding the human body, an ability used in his work of spiritual healing.

There are, too, reports of others who were rather reluctantly persuaded to visit Medjugorje, but when there found themselves convinced of Mary's presence and were filled with peace and confidence.

For many pilgrims to Medjugorje the first visit may lead to an ardent wish to return there perhaps because, as one man put it, "it takes a lot of getting used to"; or because the peace and mutual trust found there overcome all denominational, cultural and class differences in the slow realization that each and all are indeed of equal value to God.

This perhaps expresses the unerring sense of the faithful, the *sensus fidelium* of the Catholic Church which is nevertheless experienced by everyone as the instinct of believers, and can alert sceptics to become believers: it is the experience of Medjugorje which is common to all; and as Slavko has said, a gift to encourage them to go on in faith. Laurentin points out that until ordinary people recognize an authentic message, there is nothing for the Church to discern or investigate: and in von Balthasar's view the *sensus fidelium* is the uncomplicated response of the faithful, at times a genuine test of truth. Like others, he was impressed by Medjugorje's good effect on the lives of so many people of so many kinds from so many parts of the world: the good fruits from the sound tree of Matthew 7:16–20, given to those whose instinct is that Mary is there through what Bob Faricy calls a kind of mass guidance by the Holy Spirit; while God may be speaking to the world through Mary at Medjugorje, however, all prophetic messages are subject to discernment, and unauthentic elements can creep in.

David du Plessis, an American Pentecostalist Protestant, went to Medjugorje prepared to resist what he regarded as misplaced Catholic emphasis on the Virgin. Expecting to find there only Mary-worship, his experience of calm and reverent prayer centred on the Gospel showed him how Mary can lead to Christ; a manifestation to him of the Holy Spirit about which he decided to inform the Pope. Known first to the

Pentecostal Churches as "Mr Pentecost", David du Plessis's life was shaped from 1936 by the prophecy of a semi-literate Yorkshire plumber who told him, "If you are faithful and humble the Lord will use you. . .and you will see the greatest events in church history." In 1947 he began his ecumenical work by speaking to Church leaders in the U.S.A.[1] He talked about the renewal in the twentieth century of Christ's promise to the apostles before he left them: "you will be baptised with the Holy Spirit"[2] – a baptism which takes the form of a sudden joyous certainty of God, and may occur to any person at any time in any place.

This renewal had spread to all American Churches of the Protestant tradition by 1960, reaching the British Isles in 1963, when David du Plessis spoke of it as he had in America. There was a dramatic day in 1967, when a group of Roman Catholics experienced and began to spread the same message of renewal: to quote Peter Hocken (see bibliography), "Only those Christians with a knowledge of how deeply the Protestant world has suspected and opposed the Roman Catholic Church can sense what a bombshell this was"; and "Never before since the division that rent Western Christendom in the sixteenth century had Protestants and Catholics been brought into the same movement of revival and renewal". It was seen as the "new Pentecost" for which John XXIII had prayed in 1962, the more powerful because those affected were

1 Hocken (bibliography) pp. 18, 19.
2 Acts 1:5.

young, intelligent, ordinary lay-people. The Pope's prayer at the opening of the Second Vatican Council in 1962 had been

O Holy Spirit, renew your wonders in this our day, as by a new Pentecost.

One of these wonders occurred at an International Leaders' Conference of the Catholic Charismatic Renewal, held in Rome from 4 to 9 May 1981, at which Tomislav Vlasic was a delegate from Croatia, the Medjugorje district of Hercegovina. Having resigned from the Franciscan Council in Hercegovina and said

No one can do anything about the problems of the Church; all we can do is pray and wait

he asked a Canadian delegate, Father Emilio Tardif, to pray with him for the healing of the Church. As he prayed, Tardif uttered an unintelligible prophecy in the name of the Lord:

Do not fear, I am sending you my Mother

while at the same time the charismatic nun Sister Briege McKenna, author of *Miracles Do Happen*, received a prophetic vision. She saw a white church with twin steeples and in its sanctuary sat Tomislav, with water flowing from the altar and a crowd coming with cupped hands to drink from it. She was unable to get to Medjugorje until June 1985, when she recognized the church of her vision and understood the symbol of the living waters of the river of life of Revelation chapter 22, of which verse 3 reads "The curse of destruction will be abolished", and verse 10 "Do not keep the prophecies in this book a secret, because the Time is close".

Tomislav was not in Medjugorje when the Mother of God was believed to have first appeared there, or when the children claim she told them "I wish to be with you to convert and reconcile the whole world"; but he was the children's spiritual adviser from August 1981 until transferred by the bishop in September 1984.

Could this charismatic movement of the Holy Spirit, which spread to every continent and all denominations, be seen as a preliminary to Mary's call from Medjugorje for all humanity to unite in faith and love? It may be remembered that Slavko discovered the six children to have no one human leader; and in much the same way the new Pentecost had no one human founder. .

Another American who became convinced that Mary was speaking to the whole world from Medjugorje is Wayne Weible (as in "bible"), a Lutheran Protestant. Divorced and re-married, he shunned church-going as hypocritical until persuaded by his wife in 1982 to have their child baptized; by an unlikely chain of events he later found himself teaching an adult Sunday School class. In October 1985 someone suggested Medjugorje as a topic for study and Wayne took home a borrowed video-tape. As a professional journalist responsible for writing a weekly news-column, he recognized in this a good story at the right time – about the Virgin Mary and near Christmas – but he was influenced in a personal way known only to his wife; and having researched the details, he began a series of four news columns starting on 4 December.

He almost lost his nerve before publication of the first column – "it all sounded terribly religious" – but the response was good; and after the second column he agreed to meet an enthusiastic Catholic priest who had visited Medjugorje a year earlier but had failed, on his return, to persuade any news agency to publish the story. This was Father Scotti, who spoke prophetically in tongues,[3] telling Wayne that he had a message for him from Mary. "She says: you are her son. And she is asking you to write about this, but more than that: to contribute your life to it, to consecrate yourself completely to spreading the message of Medjugorje"; and he went on to prophesy broadcasting and public speaking.

Wayne was startled almost out of his wits, not only by the message but because it was a sign and corroboration of the secret he shared with his wife. On the evening they had watched the video together he had been aware of a *locution*, that inner but inaudible voice, clearly telling him

You are my son, and you are to do my Son's work. Write about the events in Medjugorje. Afterwards you will no longer be in this work (newspapers) for your life will be devoted to spreading the message. This will become your life's mission if you choose to accept it.

3 1 Corinthians 14.

By his wife's quizzical reaction when informed that the Virgin Mary had just spoken to him, he knew that these words were for him alone, yet that he was still perfectly sane; and in a state of shock, having seldom even thought of Mary before and overwhelmed by a sense of his own unworthiness, he prayed at length "Why me?". He said he was shown that by God's mercy, forgiveness and acceptance of himself he must take up this challenge, conscious for the first time of the reality of Christ and aware too that this was the same Mary who had accepted the motherhood of God without question; the Mary of whom Luther wrote in 1521, "She does not want you to come to her, but through her to God." (It was a Catholic priest in 1989 who pointed out to the author the beauty of Luther's commentary on the Magnificat, Mary's hymn of praise.)

Encouraged by Father Scotti and by the unexpected sale of his newspapers, Wayne decided to print the four columns in tabloid form, for the first time taking courage to publish the words Mary had given him. By February 1990 he informed a London audience that the tabloid had sold twenty million copies, by which time he had talked about Medjugorje in sixty other countries, chiefly to emphasize that it was not a Catholic phenomenon, but was about God's call to everyone.

He undertook the first of many visits to Medjugorje in May 1986.

In March 1990 Slavko was heard to tell another London meeting that Mary had not said that all must convert to the Roman Catholic Church nor, he was glad to say, had she spoken of unity, as this would merely have provoked more discussion.

As long as she appeared on the hillside in the natural environment which essentially belongs to everyone as part of creation, there was no doubt that her appearances were potentially of equal significance for everyone. It seems possible that this may explain her hesitation in agreeing to the children's request on June 30th that they might in future see her in the local church.

There may be many reasons for the duration of these alleged visions, from 1981 to 1991 (or longer). One such reason may be the impossibility of six people perpetrating a hoax so consistently for so long; and another the possibility that only by patient repetition will it become clear that this message, if from Christ through his Mother, is a call to all mankind to make peace and to share the rich diversity of their religious beliefs in faith and love.

3
Signs, Secrets and Healings

Most modern people resist what is implied by the word supernatural, believing that all can be explained in science or by cause and effect. The inexplicable sights verified by impartial observers in Medjugorje since 1981, quite independently of anything that the visionaries may have said, are as much of an enigma as are the healings there which have surprised or confounded the medical profession.

The Bible warns against false prophets who will arise and produce great signs and portents; yet the man to whom Christ said, "So you will not believe unless you see signs and portents!"[1] went home to find that the child he had left at the point of death had begun to recover at the moment when he was told by Jesus, "Go home, your son will live".[2] This, says St John, was the second *sign* at Cana in Galilee.

1 Matthew 24:24.
2 John 4:46–54.

There has been no dearth of signs and portents in Medjugorje since the visions began; and though it becomes increasingly clear that these are of little importance in comparison with what the visions are really about – which is belief in the existence of God leading to conversion of heart – yet there seems little doubt that the signs of God's power have helped that belief by reassuring the pilgrims. The visionaries need no reassurance.

Light, either unnaturally bright or unnaturally present, has been the source and signal of the signs; a light taken by some as corroboration of the presence and purposes of God. Could it be a manifestation in terms of 1 John 1:5, "God is light"?

There is a landmark on top of the highest mountain in the region in the form of a massive, unadorned and stark concrete cross fourteen metres high and said to weigh fourteen tons, its only embellishment a lightning conductor which deflects the storms and thus preserves the crops from damage by hail. The footpath up this mountain involves climbing round or over sharp rocky outcrops and large boulders; so that considerable labour must have been involved in carrying up, helped only by donkeys, the necessary materials which included water for mixing the concrete.

The local legend is that in early 1933, a papal Holy Year, Pope Pius XI dreamed of a cross on the highest hill in Hercegovina, which happens to be the mountain in question. The parish priest, summoned to Rome to hear of this great revelation, hurried home with the news. The people then got to work, completing the cross in March 1934 to commemorate the nineteenth centenary of the death of Christ, and changing its name from Rosehip Hill to Hill of the Cross or *Krizevac*. They looked on this hill as a calvary, a representation of the place of Christ's crucifixion, and at least once a year and always on Good Friday the local people made their way up to its summit for a celebration of the Last Supper, or Holy Communion.

Among the strange forms of light originating from Krizevac are casual references by Anglicans to the cross being floodlit at night; one layman in 1987, having satisfied himself that what he saw from the village was the effect of candles lit on the plinth of the cross, later realized that candle-power at that height and distance would be invisible.

Also in 1987, the vicar of an Anglican parish in Derbyshire was in Medjugorje with his wife and a group of pilgrims. At about 10.30 p.m. in complete darkness they proceeded by torchlight to join their son in another lodging, there to sit under a vine and enjoy the cool of the evening while looking towards Krizevac, which they were pleasantly surprised to find floodlit by a warm glow; the date was 25 July, which happens to be St James's day, patron saint of the local church. Next day enquiries established that electricity was not connected to the mountain which could not possibly, therefore, have been floodlit.

It seems undeniable that, besides the eight children, certain others were startled by the sudden sight of Mary, a fairly typical example being that of another layman — a conventional Englishman of about seventy. He was making his way alone on foot to the village from the Hill of Apparitions at dusk on a wet evening, when he was suddenly aware of a woman-shaped light "floating" past him and entering a certain house. Walking on in a state of shock, he was offered a lift by someone who turned out to be a doctor who was able to identify the house as that of the ailing Vicka, (page 79) whom she had been to visit and to whom the Virgin had just appeared.

Then there was an American Protestant pilgrim who set out in darkness at 4 a.m. to climb Krizevac before sunrise. As he walked towards the vague shape of the mountain, light suddenly shone from its summit, an experience he afterwards found was familiar to the local people who, when one saw it, would wake the others. There has been more of this sort of thing, which of course draws the seekers after sensationalism who may thereby miss the far more significant and awakening meaning to which the sign points.

But on 22 October 1981, at about 4.30 p.m. on a rainy day, something momentous indeed was observed by over seventy people in Medjugorje, who saw the cross on Krizevac obliterated by a column or pillar of bright white light, in which was clearly visible the silhouette of a woman with outstretched hands looking towards the church, her feet hidden in a luminous cloud. A priest with poor eyesight was alerted by seeing pale rose-coloured light in place of the cross until, with the help of binoculars, he was able to pick out the white silhouette. This phenomenon was first noticed by a friar who happened to glance out of a rectory window; and at his astonished shout he was joined by three of his brethren. One brought binoculars, with which in turn they all examined the woman of light, though unable to discern details of her face. The four are known by name and have left written reports of what they witnessed.

The figure remained in view for about half an hour. The four priests, who had come from the neighbouring monastery of Humac to hear confessions, accepted this appearance with great joy and as a reward for their exhausting work in the confessionals during the crowded four months since June. (It was to be some time before this work was taken on by the constant supply of secular and other priests who came as pilgrims.) But their joy was hardly less than that of the two nuns and seventy or more other people who were called out of the church to see the sight and who knelt on the wet ground oblivious of the still falling rain, their eyes on the mountain-top as they sang, shouted, prayed and wept tears of happiness. These kneeling people were joined by three priests and four nuns arriving from Split in a car, from which they had seen the figure over a mile away; though one of the nuns saw nothing, either on the journey or when she joined the people who were kneeling on the wet ground, though it is fair to assume that she would like to have done so. A common factor reported in visionary experience is an awareness of an object or person invisible to some though not all of those present. This may corroborate the evidence of the others, since it seems to rule out mass hallucination and autosuggestion. The same sort of thing occurred on 24 June at the first vision, when two of the eight children who saw Mary that day were deeply disappointed never to do so again.

When the Virgin appeared to the children and spoke to them after the phenomenon of the disappearing cross on the mountain-top, she told them that it was she herself who was there and that ''all these signs are to reinforce your faith until I send the permanent sign'' (since referred to as the ''great sign''); and in conjunction with the mysterious fire of six days later, these incidents may point to the possible truth of the children's reports of daily visits from Mary; true accounts of actual events, though inaudible and invisible to almost everyone else; visible signs of the presence of an invisible God, like the burning bush which puzzled Moses.

Although the luminous figure which took the place of the cross could have been an optical illusion due to atmospheric weather conditions, the same cannot be said of the flames of fire which broke out on 28 October 1981 on the hill of Podbrdo (Po*d* brr doe) where the eight children say they first saw the lady four months earlier. Several hundred people stood and watched this conspicuous blaze for fifteen minutes until police and firemen arrived to deal with it: but no bonfire, no brazier, no embers, no ash nor any other trace of fire could be found. That evening *Gospa* told the children that the fire was a small herald of the great sign that was to come.

Two more significant stories of light are recalled here: one that on or about 6 August 1981, spread over the night sky from Krizevac to the church, was seen the word MIR (meaning PEACE) in huge letters variously described as flame-coloured, golden, bright or of light. Discrepancies in reporting are not entirely surprising, given the shock and amazement the sight must have caused the many people who saw and compared notes about it; but that it was seen by many is not in doubt, or that no mechanical means existed to account for it: even perhaps that it was an unmistakeable sign, reassurance and illustration of Mary's main message – *"Peace to Humanity"*.

There was a most unlikely echo of this message in Ayrshire, Scotland in December 1984. A man named John Watters, driving a van home to Kilmarnock, was startled at 7.30 p.m. to see three large white marks standing out very clearly against the dark sky. It made no sense until he went to a talk about Medjugorje a week later, and realized that what he had seen were the letters MIR as though in a mirror, clearly demonstrated by a painting he made from memory.

The other story of significant light involved Marinko, the man who became a friend to the children from the second day (page 24). About three weeks after the first vision, Mary told the children to go to the same place at 11 p.m. Marinko and some forty others went with them when they then saw an opening in the sky, from which light appeared to break out and move towards the circle where they stood round a wooden cross, and where the light settled before fragmenting into thousands of little stars too bright to look at. Some wept, others screamed, including some of the children who claimed that the Virgin was in their midst praying with them, though invisible to the rest. All went home with a rather confused impression of what had really happened, though convinced that no one had been letting off fireworks; but "I'll never forget that experience," said Marinko.

The great sign, of which the mystery fire was said to be only a small herald, is the third of ten secrets which the children say they have been, or will be, given. These secrets are regarded as a vital part of the visionary message, are said to concern the future of this planet, and when all the children know all the secrets the visions will cease. So far only the two married girls, Mirjana and Ivanka, know the tenth; but all know when the great sign will appear on Podbrdo and all are determined to keep all the secrets until told otherwise by the Virgin. Many attempts, both subtle and blatant, have been made to wrest the secrets from the wary Six, but without success, a feat for which they claim unseen help; and all know the dates on which the secrets may be made public.

The arrival of the great sign – beautiful, intangible, indestructible and undeniable – is for conversion; it will be the last chance for atheists to believe, an occasion of dread for those who still reject the Gospel and of joy for those who accept it. When the sign appears it will no longer be possible to doubt that Mary was seen in Medjugorje, to warn of the existence of the omnipotent God of all creation, who calls his children to turn back from the abyss of doubt and find faith and peace, when miracles and healings will follow. Like the second coming of Christ, this great sign has been expected since it was first heard of; but in June 1983 Mary told the children that the sign *will* come, her urgent call meanwhile being for all people to convert to belief in God.

Faricy says that the messages are both prophetic and apocalyptic, the prophetic telling *us* what to do, the apocalyptic what God *intends* to do; while Laurentin points out that "the enemies of Christ were not converted by his miracles, or even by his resurrection". But as news of Christ's healing miracles spread, so the numbers of his adherents increased: and whether or not certain cures at Medjugorje are miraculous, medical doctors seem at a loss to account for them and they must be a contributory cause, apart from curiosity, of the faith and hope which draws there such vast numbers of international pilgrims.

At least twelve people, whose names are recorded by Laurentin, were moved by faith and hope to put in water some earth, herbs and flowers brought home from the place on the hill where Mary was said first to have stood. By using the resulting potion with prayer and fasting they were healed of blindness, deafness and other severe ailments. An example was the cure of a man of 85, blind and paralysed as the result of a stroke, who asked for earth and sage from the hill. Mixing this with water, he washed his face and body and could immediately see his wife; and next day was able to use his paralysed arm. This constant excavation of earth on Podbrdo has caused a small hollow, in the centre of which stands a wooden cross; and it was round this hollow that Marinko stood with the children and others when Mary came to them at 11 p.m. in the cloud of starry light described on page 46.

If this form of healing seems almost too simple to accept, or even of having possible overtones of the pagan as well as the psychosomatic, Medjugorje parish records include, besides over three hundred cures by March 1988, medically well-documented accounts of three people having complex and long-standing multiple sclerosis who were not only instantaneously cured of paralysis but were as instantly able to walk or run, using muscles long inactive. They are:

Diana Basile, Italian, married with three sons: paralysed for twelve years, blind in one eye and incontinent, who *walked* out of the apparitions room in Medjugorje after a vision on 23 May 1984.

Rita Klaus, American, married with three daughters: she had multiple sclerosis for twenty-five years, getting about in a wheelchair. In February 1986 she read about Medjugorje and on the evening of 18 June after prayer she knew she must ask for healing: the next day she could move her feet and legs and by the same evening she *ran* upstairs, quite recovered.

Agnes Heupel, German, paralysed in 1974. In 1983 she dreamed of a white church with twin towers, later recognizing it from a photograph of Medjugorje, and knew she must get there somehow. On 12 May 1986 she too *walked* out of the apparition room, cured.

During the sixth vision, in June 1981, the children begged Mary to ''make a miracle so that everyone will believe us'', asking her to heal Daniel Setka, a child of four who was mute and paralysed: they quoted her as saying, ''Let his parents believe firmly and he will be healed.'' On the way home Daniel's amazed parents heard him call for a drink as he slapped the table. By April 1983, though his right hand was less mobile than his left, he was kicking a soccer ball in the yard; his speech was not entirely clear, but he was able to make himself perfectly understood, is improving steadily and will, so his parents firmly believe, fully recover. The children say that Mary later told them, ''Only God can heal.'' It all sounds rather like St Matthew quoting Christ: ''Go back and tell what you hear and see; the blind see, the lame walk, the deaf hear, and happy is the man who does not lose faith in me.[3]''

3 Matthew 11:5.

4
The Bishop Disagrees

The attitude of Bishop Zanic, in whose diocese the alleged visions are happening, changed dramatically from one of initial encouragement or even conviction to an implacable opposition six months after the visions began. The sequence of events which brought about this change of mind and heart are concerned with Yugoslavian local history, Vatican policy and the bishop's sense of his own heavy responsibility in the matter.

In August 1980 Pavao Zanic had become only the second secular Bishop of Mostar, creating a new cathedral parish where for centuries the bishops had been Franciscans.

He had been much influenced by reports of other visions of the Virgin and had visited shrines built in honour of her appearances in Belgium and Sicily, besides leading pilgrimages to Lourdes, where he had gone no less than eight times.

During the first few weeks of the Medjugorje events and before he listened to what the children had to tell him, he asked them for a solemn promise to speak the truth in describing their experiences to him; and he is known to have gone to Medjugorje five times at the beginning, and to have wept with joy at the possibility of there being another Lourdes in his own diocese. In a recorded sermon in Medjugorje church on 25 July 1981 he said, "I am profoundly convinced that the children are not lying."

His later denunciation of these same children as liars, his determination to repress pilgrimage and all other activities connected with the Medjugorje phenomenon, and his undertaking to do penance by travelling the twenty miles from Mostar to Medjugorje on his knees should a sign of Mary's presence there ever be given, can only be understood in the context of what is known as the Hercegovina Case. This complex issue is exclusively concerned with the administration of the Roman Catholic Church in that particular part of Yugoslavia; it has cast a deep shadow over the light of the Medjugorje visions and has led to what may reasonably be described as public bickering on an international scale.

Originating in the fourteenth century and in a part of the history of Hercegovina which is touched on in chapters 9 and 10, it derives from the fact that for centuries the bishops and priests in that part of Yugoslavia had been Franciscan friars. Trouble began in 1881 after the Turkish occupation ended, when Rome decreed that thereafter secular priests – that is, not friars or monks – should share the ministry, that a bishop could dispose of the parishes as he wished and a diocese of Mostar was founded. In 1923 Rome agreed to a harmonious division of the parishes, but in 1942 when the first secular bishop was appointed, this agreement was annulled without consultation with the Franciscans, who in 1975 were told to relinquish seven parishes at once, and the rest by degrees.

The Franciscans were prepared to do this, but the plan was strongly opposed by the people who looked on the Franciscans as part of themselves, sharing their joys and sorrows as their own kin and sustaining their faith as they had through the long history of Turkish persecution; thus they resisted the newcomers as unable to understand their spiritual needs. Appeals from the Franciscans to Rome for help in resolving the difficulties were ignored.

Pavao Zanic was appointed Bishop of Mostar, the capital of Hercegovina, in 1980, when he asserted his authority by creating a new cathedral and parish which had the effect of transferring three quarters of the people into the care of secular priests. Protests followed, which included stone-throwing; and at a place called Grude some thirty miles from Medjugorje, parishioners went so far as to wall up their church doors to prevent entrance by a secular priest.

Whatever the grounds for the accusations exchanged, it seems clear that there was a good deal of mutual distrust and resentment; and if the Franciscans were hurt and humiliated by what they regarded as unjust treatment, the bishop was outraged by what he saw as flagrant disobedience to himself as Rome's representative. It is fair to add that he shows himself as a disciplinarian rather than as a shepherd of his flock.

In 1980 the bishop had transferred a Franciscan who
protested in church that this division of parishes was
not in accordance with what had been agreed. As a
further discipline he banished from the diocese two
young friars named Prusina and Vego, whose
subsequent conduct was to have a considerable
influence on the bishop's view of the authenticity or
otherwise of the visions. Though by no means the only
ones to resist deserting those who relied on them, these
two were alone in suffering the punishment of being
suspended as priests, and thus became scapegoats for
all the others. In April 1981 they were ordered to leave
Mostar, but had not done so when the visions began
in June.

The two friars had visited Medjugorje a week after
the visions began, and in October the Virgin is said
to have responded to Vego's question about
Hercegovina through the children, by saying that the
problem would be resolved through prayer and
patience. Encouraged by sympathetic parishioners and
again through the children, in December they
consulted her about their own plight. When they asked
her whether or not they should stay in Mostar, her
response caused the bishop to react with alarm and
antagonism. The crucial words attributed to Mary by
Vicka and the other children were:

23 Dec 81	The bishop is responsible. (repeated 3 Jan)
	The friars are not guilty. (repeated 3 Jan)
3 Jan 82	Let them stay. (repeated 29 Sept 82)
	The bishop does not see to it that there
	is order. It is his fault. He will not always

be bishop. The call to MIR (peace) is also addressed to the bishop.

Our Mother wants it said to the bishop that he has made a precipitous decision. Let him reflect again and listen. . .both priests are not guilty.

20 Jan 82   They are not guilty.

16 April 82 What is the matter with the bishop? (from Vicka)

(Mary) I am still waiting to know if he is going to yield soon to the message I gave him through you. (The bishop's version of this is "I am waiting for him to obey the order which I have given him through you".)

23 June 82   (from Vicka) The bishop thinks you are not the Blessed Virgin because you do not respect the decision of the leaders.

(Mary) Respect the leaders and obey them, but they also make mistakes.

17 Jan 84   The bishop thinks you are not the true *Gospa* (that is, the Mother of God). Mary replied, Pray for the bishop.

In quoting these messages at even greater length Laurentin and Lejeune point out that they were written from memory, possibly after some delay; that they are certainly coloured by the children's liking and sympathy for the two genuinely very troubled friars; and further that the children were still not adult at that time, and had acquired the habit of speaking to the Virgin as children chatter to their mothers. Indeed,

Vicka's perplexity in the matter is clear from her constant appeals to Mary for her help in understanding the problem.

In December 1981 Tomislav Vlasic – born 1946 in the neighbouring town of Citluk, who became the children's adviser after Jozo was imprisoned (page 28) – wrote in the *Parish Chronicle* that in trying to establish the content of the alleged messages to Vicka, the limitations of her own vocabulary became clear to him, and that it was necessary for him to remember that he was dealing with children.

Not until February 1983 did the bishop learn of the messages that concerned him. His immediate conviction that the alleged visions were not of Mary was based on his certainty that the Blessed Virgin would not criticize him as local bishop, that the words attributed to her were therefore an invention and that the apparitions could not possibly be authentic. He dismissed them from then onwards as collective hallucinations, cleverly exploited by the Hercegovina friars to discredit him.

He also became convinced that comments which in his view, were personally damaging, were recorded by Vicka in a "secret diary" he must somehow obtain. To reassure him Tomislav Vlasic swore on a crucifix that no such diary existed. The ensuing arguments, accusations and explanations to be found in the relevant sources make wearisome reading. Although the children may well have contradicted themselves in the rather alarming circumstances of episcopal interrogation, and Vicka did undoubtedly keep a record of some kind, it seems clear that "the (secret) diary which you think exists is non-existent", as Laurentin wrote to the bishop when protesting that certain of his statements did not conform to the truth.

If Medjugorje is about God through Mary calling all humanity to peace through love, Vatican policy and the local bishop's misinterpretation of the Pope's request in December 1981 that the matter should be resolved as soon as possible seem merely incidental. Bishop Zanic, however, sees the problem of the Two Friars as "the essential point for the understanding and acceptance of the apparitions at Medjugorje". Laurentin's view seems the more reasonable; namely, that the problem obscures the main message of Medjugorje.

So heavily did the Hercegovina Case weigh on the bishop's mind that at his first meeting with the six children in July 1981 he asked them only if the Virgin had said anything about it; and although the Case does not touch on the question of whether or not the Virgin is appearing in Medjugorje (not one of the seven remaining Franciscan parishes), for Bishop Zanic it was to become the only issue of any real importance, eclipsing any possibility of a Divine intimation to the world or to himself.

In October 1984 the bishop composed a 23-page letter, which he circulated not only to Roman Catholic bishops and institutions round the world, but also to the world's press. Entitled "The Present Position" it describes the "unwise propaganda and irresponsible organization of pilgrimages to Medjugorje", condemning the visions as false and forbidding pilgrimage on that account, with a clear implication that Rome shared his view; though this was not in fact the case, Rome having still reserved judgement.

In the letter the bishop uses misinformation and half truths to prove his point, and resorts to slander to justify his negative appraisal. He concludes that Father Tomislav Vlasic, being familiar with theology (his doctorate is in New Testament studies), had himself composed the messages, failing to mention that this friar was twenty miles away in Capljina when the visions began on 24 June and did not come to Medjugorje as the children's spiritual adviser until Jozo was imprisoned on 17 August. Tomislav is accused of being a mystifier and charismatic wizard, of perjury in denying on oath the existence of a secret diary, and of having the greatest responsibility in the real aim of the Franciscans, which is to demonstrate that they are in the right and the bishop is in the wrong. The Abbé Laurentin, who had by October 1989 visited Medjugorje twenty-one times at his own expense and is the acknowledged expert on universal visions of the Virgin, is charged with abusing his authority to make quick and easy money by his writing.

The recently deceased and world-famous Swiss theologian Hans Urs von Balthasar wrote to Laurentin that he was shocked by the slanderous attack on Tomislav Vlasic, whom he regarded as a model of humility and a true Christian man of God; and he reproached the bishop for his denigration of people who are renowned and innocent in a letter to him beginning ''My Lord, what a sorry document you have sent throughout the world.''

Archbishop Franic of Split, whose diocese adjoins

that of Mostar but to whom Zanic is not answerable, believes the visions to be genuine and noted that they had done more for the faith in three years than all Hercegovina's pastoral activity of the previous forty. In February 1985 he wrote to Cardinal Ratzinger in Rome that the Bishop of Mostar is

> so convinced that he is persecuted by the friars of Medjugorje as to behave accordingly: it is said, in fact, in good and sure conscience that, driven by his persecution mania, he will be satisfied only when he succeeds in declaring the facts of Medjugorje unauthentic.

The archbishop ends this letter by begging Rome to appoint an International Commission to examine "the difficulties which so seriously and dramatically upset the mind of His Excellency Bishop Zanic".

The bishop's disturbed mind was also observed by Slavko and two other friars at a meeting of 31 October 1984, in which he said that all the children were lying to him and hiding Vicka's diaries; and if the friars would say that the *Gospa* is blaspheming the bishop, people will stop coming.

His determination to deny the healings (chapter 3) or to refuse to recognize in them the sign chosen by Christ, perhaps emphasizes his closed mind to everything but his own pain.

Bishop Zanic had himself convened two commissions of inquiry in early 1982 and 1984. In January 1985 he informed Robert Faricy S.J., who had written of Medjugorje and who was at that time

Professor of Spirituality at the Gregorian University
in Rome, that the judgement of events would not come
from the commission but from himself, and that he had
already decided that the Virgin was certainly not
appearing in Medjugorje. A National Inquiry
Commission was appointed in January 1987, an
unprecedented occurrence in the Roman Catholic
Church, where investigation of alleged apparitions has
always been the responsibility of the diocese and
bishop concerned: the decision was made in April 1986
as a result of the proposed negative judgement of
Bishop Zanic, who was then asked to dissolve his own
second inquiry.

Undaunted, and unwavering in his condemnation
of the Franciscans, at a confirmation in Medjugorje
church on 25 July 1987 the bishop's sermon to a
shocked congregation included the words "To preach
to the blessed people of the faithful the lie about God,
Jesus, and the Blessed Virgin deserves the bottom of
hell".

On 29 January 1982 Prusina and Vego were
dismissed from the Franciscan Order for disobedience
to the bishop and to Rome. Knowing such expulsion
to be contrary to canon law, their appeal to the
Supreme Ecclesiastical Tribunal in Rome was expected
to succeed by the end of 1986, but the appeal was
curtailed. Vego then left the priesthood and got
married. Prusina was assigned to Austria but, unable
to speak German, was transferred to Dubrovnik. But
by 1988 that diocese was also administered by Zanic,
who informed Laurentin that he had forbidden
Prusina every ministry, not only in the diocese of

Dubrovnik but wherever it might be in the world.

As a man in spiritual crisis who complains, furthermore, that news of The Virgin's appearance has disturbed the peace of his diocese, Bishop Zanic deserves much compassion; and as Angelo Bena points out, opposition may achieve more than enthusiasm in establishing the truth.

Since the fifteenth century the role of Devil's Advocate or promoter of the faith (Promotor Fidei) has been critically to examine the virtues of an alleged miracle, so that rash decisions may be avoided. It seems that the Bishop of Mostar most ably fulfils this function.

5
Further Opposition

A book entitled *The Hidden Side of Medjugorje*, written
in French and published in Canada, appeared in an
English translation in 1989. The author, Ivo Sivric, was
born and brought up in Medjugorje, finishing his
education in Mostar and Rome and becoming a
Franciscan priest before emigrating to the U.S.A. In
1983 aged sixty-six, two years after the Virgin's first
appearance there, he returned to Medjugorje for the
first of three annual visits to assess and comment upon
what was happening in his native village. He seems
to regard himself as uniquely qualified to do so, though
his reasons for this are not entirely clear since there
is nothing to support his contention that he alone
understands the psychology, background and
characteristics of the six visionary children; indeed, two
friars ministering in Medjugorje in 1990 were both born
a few miles away in Humac.

He had, however, published in Chicago in 1982 *The
Peasant Culture of Bosnia and Hercegovina*; and his book
on Medjugorje is a large, painstaking and scholarly
work, quoting from over two hundred sources and

with three hundred and seventy notes and seventeen appendices.

It is edited by Louis Bélanger, who teaches in the theology department at Montreal University as a specialist in paranormal phenomena (though without a doctorate), and concedes that his interpretation of the events has no religious basis. He considers the alleged appearances of Mary to be no more than the manifestation of a mediumistic entity peddling gossip, an aspect of the visions which he says has been cunningly suppressed by Laurentin, whom he vilifies relentlessly. The book's purpose, he states, is to expose the contradictions, ambiguities and misleading conduct implicit in favourable accounts; and he recognizes the author's disquiet at the credibility of the Catholic Church in this affair, fearing that she will emerge from it bruised and discredited in public opinion. It may be deduced that he has little confidence in the caution and discernment of the Pope or his satellites in the matter.

At first glance this book is impressive, appearing to make a good case for doubting the authenticity of the Medjugorje events, particularly for those who may not be familiar with the facts. But a closer examination discloses misrepresentation of those facts, and what a barrister has defined as masterly manipulation of the source documents in a sustained attempt to obscure the truth and present a contrary case.

It is a disturbing book, therefore, and also a sad one; sad because the reader becomes aware of how deeply Sivric may have regretted his forty-year exile in the U.S.A. and, even more, his absence from Medjugorje when the visions began. The Sivric family are well represented in Medjugorje though some at least of its members are not familiar with the contents of "Uncle Ivo's" book, since they have no knowledge of the French or English languages and little curiosity about it.

Sivric is influenced by his upbringing in a house near Medjugorje church, and by his remaining family and friends there. He claims to be well acquainted with his brother Franciscans and with the six children, all of whom he describes as the "actors", though according to Rupcic and Foley he neither questioned the children nor was he present at any time or place during their claimed visions. Further, he failed to interview direct witnesses such as Jozo Zovko, or to consult the parish staff and records.

He relied for information on his family and on people who were opposed to what was happening, whose identity he found it necessary to protect so that they would not be banished from the village; a rather ambiguous statement. Was the information extracted only under oath of secrecy? Who might banish them – the friars, the Communists, their neighbours, the pilgrims? And if, as he says, they felt bound in conscience to disclose certain disquieting facts, who or what had deterred them and why had they not done so? There is a cloak and dagger innuendo, an implication of a terrorized minority who dare not speak, in his assertion that in him they found an ally and attentive confidant. To anyone who has wandered casually about the village and farms or accepted hospitality from the smiling inhabitants this seems an absurd caricature of the reality.

In dismissing as slanted and superficial the majority

of books and articles written about Medjugorje, Silvric clearly includes those by the Abbé Laurentin, respected theologian, author and renowned authority on visions of Mary. In his sweeping condemnation he affects to uncover a sinister campaign whose purpose is to prove the possible authenticity of the visions.

Sivric asserts that his goal in writing is to seek to establish the truth. He is, however, challenged in this by another friar, Ljudevit Rupcic, a New Testament scholar who was present at the Medjugorje events from the beginning and was the first to publish an account of them. In his monograph of October 1988 *The Great Falsification* (Sivric's book was first published in French in 1988), Rupcic claims that in casting doubt on the truth of the visions, what Sivric really seeks is the justification of his once respected family and their defence against the ostracism to which they were subjected as members of the Communist Party.

Chiefly involved were a nephew who had been promoted to a position of importance and a girl-cousin, both formerly practising Christians and both employed by the (Communist) government to investigate and suppress the visions, since assembly of crowds might lead to a recurrence of the nationalist, religious and political insurrections which had occurred before 1945 (see chapters 11 and 12).

As a native of Medjugorje, the nephew was sent to deal with what was thought to be the root of the trouble; and it was thus he who helped to harass the children, requested Jozo as parish priest to close the church and leave the district, and put pressure on the local church council to see that this was done. The cousin was one of the social workers employed to prevent the children being present for Mary's appearance on 30 June, the sixth day (page 26) and although Sivric maintains that his cousin Mica was a practising Christian at the time, parish records do not support this assertion.

The original cassette tapes of Fr Jozo's conversations with the Six during the first seven days were entirely clear and complete, but with other vital records were removed by the police (page 25) and never recovered, despite even the bishop's best endeavours; so that the tapes quoted by Sivric two or more years later were copies of copies made by various people for their own purposes, and are very far from clear; Rupcic notes that certain conversations have been deleted by cutting the tapes, parts of which are indecipherable. These deficiencies are acknowledged by Sivric at the beginning of his appendix 5 with the words, in italics *''? (incomprehensible) When it is impossible to identify the person speaking or his words, I will indicate it this way.''* The word incomprehensible recurs at least thirty-six times in appendix 16 alone; but what seems even more incomprehensible is his incontestable failure to have consulted the still living original primary sources before his critical comment.

Mica's specific function of keeping the children from Podbrdo is concealed, and the voice of her colleague Ljubica is hardly heard.

It seems clear that the object of quoting selected parts of these tapes is to emphasize Mica's charm and innocence, the inaccuracies of the Virgin's reported messages and the duplicity of the friars, of whom all are liars and Tomislav Vlasic is the greatest.

Certain inferences may be drawn, however, from these recordings of conversations between the clergy and children during the first week of the visions, that is 24 to 30 June 1981. For example, the children's dislike of the jostling crowds from which it was becoming impossible for them to escape, and their obvious longing to be by themselves on the hill with Mary; Jozo's constant efforts to persuade them to abandon the hill and go instead to the church; and Mary's apparent hesitation when asked by Mirjana if they might go to the church rather than to the hill – a hesitation already noted on page 39.

Jozo's uncertainty and indecision are very evident; and it is significant that Sivric elected to conclude the reported recordings on 30 June, two days before the experience which convinced Jozo that the children were speaking the truth, but the day on which they are quoted (from the deficient and "incomprehensible" tapes) as telling Jozo that the Virgin had said that she would appear to them three more times, and that they knew the visions would end on Friday 3 July. Thus Sivric elaborates on his hypothesis (unproved) of *Three More Times* as contrary evidence for the apparitions.

From the reliable sources of Rupcic, O'Carroll, Pelletier, Sereny and Craig the facts appear to be as follows.

On 24 June 1981 when the visions began Father Jozo Zovko was in Zagreb. He returned to his parish of Medjugorje on Saturday 27 June, questioned the children, established that they knew nothing of previous appearances of the Virgin and lent to Mirjana, the best educated, a book about Lourdes where Mary had appeared in 1858. To them all he gave rosaries and prayer books.

The book was read and discussed by the children amongst themselves, from which they concluded that as Mary had appeared to Bernadette of Lourdes eighteen times they might expect the same; they calculated on 30 June that her visits would therefore end on 3 July, after three more visits. On 4 July they did not meet on the hill; but at the usual time of the vision, in or about their own homes, Mary came to each of them separately. Thereafter the Virgin appeared to them as a group or separately wherever they might be.

Sivric's version differs. He claims Medjugorje to be a false imitation of Lourdes; he prefaces the quotation of Three More Times with the word *only*; he suggests, with great subtlety, that it is possible for Mirjana to have read a book on Lourdes ''a short time before having the visions''; and following a probable misquotation, he then says that (i.e. Jozo is a liar):

> Father Zovko ought to have remembered that he never gave the visionaries either a book on Lourdes or a Bible on June 30 1981 or earlier.

But he concedes that Mirjana had in fact read a book on Lourdes, and that she was given it by a married lady *née* SIVRIC who, says Rupcic, ''denies that she ever had any book about Lourdes''.

Few of Sivric's other criticisms can withstand close study. Though claiming Vicka as a fifth or sixth cousin, he appears to regard his failure to wrest any secrets from her or the others as proof of their deception, further demonstrated by evidence that they have contradicted themselves on several occasions; though little allowance is made for the likely effects of the merciless and almost continuous interrogation to which they had then been subjected for six years or more.

Mirjana says that Mary has kept a promise to visit her each year on her birthday, 18 March, after she had received the tenth secret in December 1982; but she is condemned by Sivric as undeserving of attention and lacking in humility for speaking of this.

The phenomena of fire and light are explained as mere illusion. Sivric knows the names of various boys who lit fires on the hill for fun; and he has been familiar since childhood with the atmospheric conditions which account for the rest though "those who knew the origin of these 'Miraculous' lights. . .did not dare say anything", presumably because they fear the wrath of the remaining 95% or more of the villagers (who must also have been aware of this deception) should their concerted conspiracy be discovered and the investigations of dedicated theologians and medical doctors be brought to nought.

Sivric is grieved to discover that the visionaries are not without faults, though "one expects that those who communicate with the *Gospa* are considered to be exemplary Christians". Why this is to be expected and by whom is not clear; but it is not too difficult to guess which of their "fellow citizens reproached them for being unfriendly". In fact, one of the more compelling reasons for believing their story is the very ordinariness of the Six, who were immature and whose rather basic education lacked any teaching on theology. They have never understood why they were chosen, unless to show that all are called; and they accept that they are no better or worse than any others.

Rupcic considers that when Rome rejected Zanic's negative findings he pursued his case against Medjugorje through Sivric, who collaborated closely with him. Sivric's rather humourless insistence on the relevance of his consanguinity with some of those concerned seems a curious motive for the time, trouble and expense involved and perhaps, like the bishop, he deserves compassion. Due to criticism and financial problems, the publication of Volume II of his book has been delayed.

6
The Children Grow Up

Slavko said that he was surprised, in January 1982, to find the Six to be so dissimilar, to have no obvious leader, and to make no effort to convince him that something extraordinary was happening. This state of affairs appeared unchanged nine or more years later.

They still met as a group whose only common interest was the daily vision and they still told him daily ''We see the *Gospa*'' – that is, the Virgin Mary. But they were no longer children, nor had they known for nine years what it was to have much private life. The three who are enabled to give totally of their time and strength to the work of being available to pilgrims are probably Vicka, Marija and Ivan. With the exception of Jakov, who was 19, they were all aged 25 to 27 in the summer of 1990. Mirjana and Ivanka were both married.

The Six are all, however, constant and consistent in their story and in obedience to Mary's wish that they should decline offers of money or other rewards which might give them either luxury or material wealth.

Bishop Zanic criticized the fact that their language

changed as a result of being coached by the friars in how to deal with doctors and journalists, when at first they had spoken like peasants. Yet they must surely have needed help in coming to terms with continual interrogation by strangers during their free time from school, and with the invasion of their quiet lives of simple country pursuits and agricultural labour. Even so, nine years later it was still necessary to correct their grammar when transcribing the Virgin's messages.

In June 1981 the youngest boy was ten. The ages of the other five varied between fifteen and seventeen, perhaps the most receptive time for maturing youth.

The children were either still at school, compulsory from the age of seven for the ensuing eight years, or if over fifteen they were undergoing a three year course to fit them for an occupation or for university. In June 1981 they were older and certainly better educated than Bernadette of Lourdes, who was illiterate and to whom Mary appeared in 1858; or than other visionary children in Portugal, Belgium and Spain in this century. Nevertheless they may be counted among the simple, the mere children, to whom the Lord of heaven and earth chose to reveal the Good News of the Gospel of Christ.[1]

For them it was good news indeed, and they say that they look forward with joy to Mary's appearances to them, and experience intense happiness in her presence and in their talks with her. They regard her as their heavenly Mother in a way which does not detract from their affection for their earthly mothers.

1 Matthew 11:25.

While their descriptions of their encounters with her and of her teaching sometimes read a little like a fairy tale, they are perhaps credible in the context of the children's steadfastness in the telling of it.

IVANKA, born on 21 April 1966, though not the eldest of the Six, was the first to say that she saw the figure of a woman wearing a crown and holding a baby, in bright light on the hill near the road. Without hesitation she cried ''Look! The Madonna'', to the mockery of her companion Mirjana. She was also the first to speak to the vision; very afraid, but also very happy.

It was Ivanka, grieving for the death of her mother in hospital two months earlier, to whom Mary said, ''Your mother is well. She is with me'' (page 22).

Ivanka's father is one of many local men who are migrant workers in Germany, where they can make a better living than on their land, and earn a far better retirement pension than at home; she has an elder brother and a younger sister. She is pretty and smiling, her manner shy and modest; her reply and that of Vicka and Mirjana when asked by Laurentin why Our Lady appeared to her, was, ''She said it's not always necessary to look for the best''. Mary told her that she is accepted as she is; and that people of all religions are accepted by Christ.

This last statement may be an oversimplification, causing concern to committed Christians. It implies the indifferentism referred to on page 30. A possible interpretation, however, may be that Mary is asking that *all* shall turn to Christ, who will welcome them.

Mary gave her the tenth and last secret on 6 May

1985, after a vision during which three of the others
were present. The next day, alone in her home as Mary
had asked, the wonder and beauty of the hour during
which they were together fully compensated for
Ivanka's sense of great loneliness at the realization that
her daily visions were over. In a written account for
Father Slavko she recorded that Mary came to her with
two angels. All were very beautiful and were clothed
with an effect of gold and silver light; and when Ivanka
was asked to express a wish, her earthly mother again
appeared and kissed her, saying how proud of her she
was.

Mary then told Ivanka that though this was their last
meeting, she must not be sad or think that she had
done anything wrong; and that she would see Mary
again every year on 25 June, the date on which they
had first spoken together. She thanked Ivanka for
cooperating with Christ's plans and asked her to be
happy because she, Mary, was her loving Mother. She
was asked to tell her friends, ''My Son and I are always
near when they call us''; and she was reminded that
she must keep the secrets until told that she might
reveal them.

Ivanka is too shy to be available to the pilgrims, her
work being to be constant in prayer and to help her
grandmother.

In December 1982 Mary suggested to the Six that
they might become monks or nuns, but that they were
free to choose. Ivanka already knew that she would
prefer marriage; and her wedding on 28 December
1986, after much reflection, was to Raiko Elez aged 25.
They had been friends before the apparitions began,

and Raiko remained constant. Their daughter Christina was born on 11 November 1987, but this did not prevent Ivanka from fasting on bread and water during the whole of Lent 1988. Their second child, a boy named Josip, arrived on 14 June 1990. From her choice of married life and motherhood it may be deduced that she can face the future with equanimity, however dire she may know the disclosure of the secrets to be.

She has travelled in Italy, France and Scotland.

MIRJANA, born 18 March 1965, was the one who ridiculed her friend Ivanka's cry of ''Look! The Madonna'' when the Virgin first appeared to them.

She is the most mature of the six and the only one to become a graduate: like the others, she is quite normal. She has one brother and lives with her parents in Sarajevo when not visiting her grandmother in Medjugorje. In her life of faith she prays for and contends with the unbelief, worldliness and materialism of a great city, whereas the other five are sustained by the praise, awe and joy which are in the very air of Medjugorje.

She and Ivanka are the only two to know all the secrets. The tenth was entrusted to Mirjana on Christmas Day 1982, when Mary said that her regular appearances to her would cease; news which caused Mirjana great grief. She could hardly believe that the happiness of help and advice in the daily visits of this beautiful, loving and merciful Mother were to end. At the time that Mary used to come to her she locked herself in her room, sad, silent, withdrawn and immersed in prayer that the vision would return. She was consoled only by Mary's promise of coming to her again every year on her birthday, 18 March, and at times of crisis in her personal life; but having chosen to work on her degree course, Mirjana understood that by her absence Mary was obedient to her own part in carrying out God's plan.

Mirjana, as the most mature of the Six, was the first to learn to live without the sweet solace of the Virgin's daily visible presence, and in due time to help the others to do so.

In some of her messages, to be discussed later, the Virgin has spoken of the activity of the devil. In June 1982, while waiting in her room for Mary's visit, Mirjana said that this personification of evil – hideous, terrifying and mocking – appeared to her instead of Mary, offering her success in love and life if she would abandon God and the Virgin, who had brought her only hardship. This is an experience common to many of the saints, and notably to the Anglican visionary Dorothy Kerin;[2] and indeed to Christ's own temptation in the wilderness.[3]

When Satan vanished Mary appeared, to tell the shaken Mirjana that this had been a necessary trial to demonstrate the devil's attempts to deflect the faithful from God's protection. If this account is true the incident has certain implications worth very serious consideration.

In July 1987, at a public audience in Rome, Archbishop Franic introduced Mirjana to the Pope,

2 *Mother of Nations*, chapter 4.
3 Gospels of Matthew, Mark and Luke.

who told her that he prayed daily for a good solution concerning Medjugorje.

As the one through whom the secrets are to be revealed, Mirjana holds a key position among the Six. On 27 June 1985 she said that she had been asked to choose a friar who would publish the secrets; and at the end of August that year his name was given as Father Peter Ljubicic. This priest, who takes the matter calmly, undertook to read the first secret still unknown to all but the Six from a paper to be given him by Mirjana. He will then pray and fast for seven days, after which he will reveal each secret event three days before it is to occur.

Are there ten or sixty secrets? Whether each visionary's ten secrets are identical is in doubt, but it seems clear that the content of the first three secrets are common to all and known by all and that all know the date on which the third, or Sign, will appear on Podbrdo as proof of the visions. Those unbelievers who have not by then heeded Mary's plea to turn to God will be bitterly sorry.

The first secrets of calamitous events are warnings, the delay in announcing the secrets being therefore regarded as merciful. Slavko is quoted as saying that Mary did not come to announce catastrophes, but to help us avoid them.

Mirjana sees her main responsibility as keeping the secrets until she is to disclose them to Father Peter. Besides her birthday visions, Mary speaks to her in interior locutions – the inner and recognized voice, though inaudible.

On 16 September 1989 she was married to Marco

Soldo, a fellow university student of economics, and a nephew of Father Slavko Soldo who now looks after a New York parish; he is also Father Slavko Barberic's nephew.

Mirjana's daughter Marija was born on 9 December 1990.

VICKA, born 3 July 1964, had failed a mathematics examination, and was at a summer school in Mostar on 24 June 1981 before getting home in a hot and crowded bus. She decided to rest, and awoke to find a note from her friends Ivanka and Mirjana asking her to join them for a walk on the hill. When she did so she reacted with panic to their call to come quickly and see the Madonna: kicking off her shoes so as to run faster, she raced for home.

The eldest of the six, she is an extrovert; outspoken, impetuous, cheerful and a good communicator. During the first week she was among the visionaries who stood on Marinko's terrace at the foot of the hill, repeating until almost midnight to the waiting crowd below her what Mary had told the Six. In May 1990, from the terrace of her parents' house near Podbrdo, she was imparting the same information daily, sometimes from 6 a.m. onwards, with unflagging energy and smiling patience, an interpreter at her side to convey the message in the language of each succeeding group of world-wide pilgrims.

Apart from the bishop's accusations concerning her ''secret diary'' (page 56) she has endured much spiritual and physical pain with equanimity if not joy, regarding it as her privileged vocation to do so.

Restored to full health in September 1988, she seems never to have questioned the Virgin's clear call as to what was God's will for her. In September 1981 Mary asked her to leave school to stay at home and look after Jakov, who was still at primary school; she is therefore the only one of the Six to have been constantly in Medjugorje since the visions began.

By December 1982 she had decided to become a nun. She is one of eight children whose father has worked in Germany for many years; her mother and grandmother are now supportive, having initially forbidden her to speak of the visions through dread of gossip and banter.

The Virgin has given details of her earthly existence to all the children; but from 7 January 1982 until 10 April 1985 she recounted to Vicka the story of her life. Although this has happened before to two nuns who were mystics – the Spanish Mary of Agreda (1602–65) and the German Catherine Emmerich in 1821, besides the mystical writer Maria Valtorta who died in 1961 in Italy, it is unlikely that Mary was physically present to them as she was to Vicka, though understood by all the others in visions. Vicka says that she was instructed by Mary to keep a careful record of this Life and to show it to no one but a certain unnamed priest (who has accepted the responsibility) on a date she will be given.

Concurrently with this writing, Vicka began to suffer in early 1982 from a series of painful and exhausting illnesses, the worst symptoms being fainting attacks and excruciating headaches thought to be caused by a brain cyst. She spent much of the time at home in a coma, but always woke a few minutes before Mary's unfailing daily appearances to her, when she was again smiling and happy. The few people with her at these times observed that as a preliminary to the daily visions she began to say the Lord's prayer for the second time, becoming silent after the petition "thy will be done", when she was in ecstasy. She afterwards explained that it was then that Mary appeared to her.

Frequent visits to a medical clinic in Zagreb failed to diagnose the trouble, though specialists noted no neurotic or psychotic symptoms; and by 1987 they concurred in the view that the complaint was spiritual rather than physical. Vicka resisted her mother's plea to ask Mary for healing, saying she knew that many souls were benefiting from her pain.

With the debilitating effects of her physical condition went the spiritual deprivation of Mary's visits at certain times, a loss accepted voluntarily by Vicka on 6 January 1985 for a period of fifty days. Mary asked of her a triple task, the nature of which is unknown to any but herself, accomplished in secrecy as she was seen to come and go alone to Krizevac and Podbrdo. The headaches and coma left her, and there was a joyous reunion with Ivan and Marija when she was able to rejoin them in February for the daily vision.

She wept at the gravity of the ninth secret, given to her in April, and on 24th of that month she accepted another undertaking during a new forty-day break in Mary's visits to her, which recommenced on 4 June. On 7th June Mary came to comfort and console her in hospital, as she recovered from an appendix operation; and when investigating her throat, the surgeons found there a swab left when her tonsils were removed.

The third task and interruption to Vicka's visions occurred from 24 August to 20 October 1986 when, during a most happy reunion, Mary thanked her for her cooperation in fulfilling with enthusiasm what she knew to have been asked of her. The headaches and coma continued, however, until in January 1988 the Virgin absented herself for a final fifty days, telling Vicka secretly that her trials would end on 25 September. Vicka wrote this information confidentially for Father Bubalo, a local priest, who sealed it in an envelope which he opened on 25 September; and on that date, most surprisingly, she recovered her health and the headaches and comas left her.

She had borne her burden without complaint, continuing to smile and speak to pilgrims as she knew Mary wished her to, until pain and exhaustion forced her to seek refuge alone in her room; but she is not yet permitted to speak of the reason for this suffering.

She may dread the tenth secret signalling the end of Mary's visits; but meanwhile she greets the pilgrims tirelessly and lays her hands on them if they think this will help them, as indeed it does; she signs their autographs; and she accepts their written pleas to God for his mercy. When she gives private interviews her sparkling eyes, ready smile and warmth of manner proclaim a very happy young woman. She says that she wants nothing in the world but her present calling.

She has travelled to Europe and the Holy Land.

IVAN, born 25 May 1965, had encountered Vicka when

she ran home without her shoes. He was picking up windfall apples, surprised that she should be scared to return to the hill; but when he saw what had transfixed the others, he too raced for home. Marinko, the man who was to protect the children from the crowds, heard the story from Vicka as he gave her a lift next morning. He decided to check with Ivan, a sensible boy, and it was Ivan's corroboration of Vicka's improbable story that made him take it seriously.

Unlike Vicka, Ivan is an introvert; serious, solitary and so shy that as a child he even avoided his own age-group, making his present assurance and his calm and confident manner with the pilgrims the more remarkable. School examinations never came easily to him, and he is content to help farm his father's tobacco and vines. One of four children, he enjoys sport and is wise rather than clever.

His mother had persuaded him to stay at home on day four when the others were taken by the police for medical tests, returning in time to go to Podbrdo without him; and as Ivan stood forlorn and alone near the foot of the hill Mary appeared to him there, saying "Peace". Having by then found a rosary in his trousers pocket, his anxious mother began to relax.

At this time his ambition was to become a priest, and in August 1981 he began training near Sarajevo as a Franciscan seminarian, transferring after a year to a Jesuit seminary in Dubrovnik. During this time, discreetly and unknown to his fellows, Mary came to him regularly. Mocked as a visionary, backward academically, and with hopes crushed, it was for him a time of great desolation.

His unhappiness was compounded while still at the first seminary when two members of the bishop's first commission demanded from the children a written statement about the Sign. Having consulted the Virgin they all refused; but on 9 May 1982, faced without warning by his Superior and the Bishop's Commissioners, Ivan put a note in a sealed envelope and handed it over. On 7 March 1985 the envelope was opened by three Commissioners, who read ''The Blessed Virgin has said she will leave a Sign. There will be a great shrine in Medjugorje in honour of her apparitions there''.

Mary reproved Ivan for writing anything under such duress; and when Slavko sought him at home, he was astonished to be greeted with ''But it isn't the Sign and I didn't reveal the date.'' Weeping with remorse, Ivan explained that Mary had warned him of Slavko's coming. Whatever the Sign may be, the great shrine seems a certainty, though he said later that when pressure was put on him he had ''said anything''.

During his year of compulsory military service between June 1986–7 Ivan distinguished himself by winning a 500-metre race, for which he was awarded eight days' leave of absence. He elected to take it at Christmas so as to be present at Ivanka's wedding in December. Self-effacing as ever, he managed to evade the waiting photographers until he had changed out of uniform. The army gave him maturity, self-confidence and new friends; and he was encouraged by being told on arrival that if his calling caused him trouble he was to say so; a rather more compassionate appraisal by a Communist commandant than that of his seminary superiors. There was no trouble, and he was given permission to leave barracks most evenings, when Mary came to him; and he was able to hear her in locutions when he prayed.

From this new self-reliance Ivan's calling became clearer to him.

One evening in July 1982 he was with a few of his own friends on Podbrdo when Mary appeared to him. They decided spontaneously to pray together, thus originating what became a very significant prayer group, unique because it was led by Mary herself.

She asks them to pray for the fulfilment of her plans for the world as well as for themselves saying, in August 1988, that she wants their cooperation and can do nothing without them. This group, never more than 15 strong, meets twice a week from 10 p.m. to midnight, every Monday on Podbrdo, every Friday on Krizevac, all the year round regardless of weather; and Krizevac under snow can be extremely cold. Some of its members travel over 30 miles each way, and when the meetings became known huge crowds joined them. In May 1990, arriving on Podbrdo as a meeting was ending, a party of four sat by the path as the returning pilgrims, some with torches, filed past in the dark. Two or three abreast on the stony path, the column descended for over an hour, singing and praying quietly in many languages; a supremely happy family of possibly a thousand people.

This prayer group has provided an example and incentive for the beginnings of many others throughout the world; Slavko is said by Laurentin to have counted 500 in Austria by May 1988.

Ivan's future vocation is known only to himself and the Virgin. Meanwhile he gives every morning to speaking of her with calm confidence to the pilgrims who flock to his parents' house to hear him, a good part of the day to helping his father farm the land, and several hours to being present in the church. In October 1990 he visited President Bush in the U.S.A.

Knowing he will see Mary, he wakes with indescribable happiness; having seen her, he sleeps in peace, and he wants nothing in his life but to go on testifying to her presence and to her messages from God.

MARIJA, born 1 April 1965, was not present on the first day when her younger sister Milka and the older Ivan saw the Virgin, to their sorrow, for the only time (page 21). This fact is regarded by enthusiasts as corroboration of the truth of what the others say, since it is clear that these two deeply regret seeing Mary once only. On the second evening Vicka agreed to call Marija if there was a vision, because she wanted to be with them even if she herself saw nothing. In fact she saw first a vague outline and then the lady's face, before they all flew up the rocky and thorny hill with a speed and ease which mystified the onlookers (page 23).

On the third evening, after the lady had told the children that she was the Blessed Virgin, she appeared to Marija alone (page 25) and from that moment Marija committed herself to Mary the Mother, who wept for the hurts of all her children and called them to make peace with God and each other. It was probably then that Marija knew that she would eventually become a nun, and only later that she thought of entering a Franciscan convent when the visions ceased. After seeing Mary's tears, she sought only Christ's purpose for her life, telling Laurentin that she thought the Six must be the happiest people on earth to have been given this message of healing, prayer and penance by the Virgin.

Marija lives with her parents, and has three brothers and two sisters; she was apprenticed to a hairdresser when the visions began. She is the most serene of the Six, by temperament uncomplicated; simple, dignified, calm, discreet, shy yet confident, her innate goodness is apparent. She gives generously of her time and strength to the pilgrims, with a consequent need for silent meditation alone, sometimes at sunrise on Krizevac.

Like Ivanka and Ivan and because Mary had asked it for them, she is tirelessly available to speak and listen to pilgrims; and since many who bring her their problems are Italians, she learned their language. Without her mentioning it as an option, many of them flocked to confession after long intervals, including some non-Catholics for the first time, one of whom was surprised to find that confession was as simple as finding the courage to say how many of the commandments he had failed to keep (nine out of ten) and how light-hearted he felt afterwards.

In 1984 it became known that the Virgin wished to give a weekly message to the parish of Medjugorje. This was transmitted by Marija every Thursday from 1 March, whether or not she was in Medjugorje, until

8 January 1987. From then onwards Marija was given these messages only on the 25th of each month, the anniversary of her first vision; but they were intended for the whole world. She told Laurentin that the messages remain in her memory, and she is able to write them out at once – for immediate translation into several languages, the words being heard only by her even if other visionaries are present. She is also given messages on Mondays and Fridays when she takes part in Ivan's prayer group on the hills; and though Ivan decided in April 1989 that these particular messages to them would no longer be published, huge crowds still attend them after dark on Podbrdo and Krizevac.

A series of seeming coincidences took Marija to the U.S.A. for the messages of November, December and January 1988–9.

Returning home in August from visits to Rome and to shrines in Portugal, Spain and France, she found her married brother Andrea critically ill from kidney failure. By then fluent in Italian, and knowing doctors in Milan (chapter 7), Marija went there for advice concerning a kidney transplant for her brother, offering herself as donor; but she was warned of both medical and financial difficulties. She then consulted an American friend who had arrived in Medjugorje for a second visit on 16 November; this was Terry Colafrancesco, director of an organization called CARITAS which existed to support pilgrimage to Medjugorje. He offered immediately to take both Marija and Andrea to the U.S.A.

The difficulties began to vanish away.

A newspaper bought on chance at Belgrade airport on 19 November informed Terry that in his home-city of Birmingham, Alabama, there was a hospital renowned for successful kidney transplants. The money was promised by a doctor in Louisiana; the family blood groups were right; and finally the operation on 16 December was successful.

During medical tests in America, ending on 6 December when Marija went home to fetch her brother's wife and child, the Virgin's daily visits to her continued, but at Medjugorje not at U.S.A. time. Her only message for a month after the operation was on 25 December, though she continued to see the Virgin daily. She also claimed that while anaesthetised for three hours, the *Gospa* was present to encourage her.

Ivan also happened to be in America that November, to see an uncle and to record a TV interview in, of all places, Birmingham, Alabama, where he too saw Mary daily.

Despite or possibly because of his visionary sister, Andrea was not among the most convinced by the Virgin's alleged appearances in his village, which he had left to work in Germany; but since his recovery from certain death and moved by his sister's selfless act of love, he now holds a different view and is building a pilgrim's house in Medjugorje.

After convalescence in Milan, Marija returned home on 22 March. Her fasting meant that it was several more weeks before she was strong enough to resume her work with the pilgrims. In November 1990 she visited President Gorbachev in Moscow.

JAKOV, born 3 June 1971, was with Marija when Vicka called to her on the second evening, before they all flew straight up the hill with such astonishing speed; and when they reached the Lady and fell to their knees, it was Jakov who was found to have knelt unscathed in a thorn bush. From that day he became one of the Six who were to claim that they saw the *Gospa* almost daily, either in Medjugorje or wherever they happened to be.

Jakov is the youngest by five to seven years; yet far from the normal teenage reaction of being bored by a boy of ten tagging along, the others accepted him from the first.

A typical boy, Jakov aged ten was lively, fidgety and a practical joker. His main interests were and are pop music and football; so that his open-mouthed absorption and intensity while in ecstasy, so apparent in photographs and while observed, is therefore in striking contrast to his normal restless behaviour and would be difficult for a boy of his age and temperament to fake or maintain. Throughout the visions, all six appear to be in this state of mystical ecstasy, discussed in the next chapter.

Jakov was one of the three visionaries with Ivanka in May 1985 when she was given the last secret. The vision remained only two minutes with the others, who were quite alarmed when they stood up to see the still-kneeling Ivanka in ecstasy for a further six minutes. It was their first sight of someone in the mystical state they had themselves so often experienced.

After Jozo's arrest on 17 August 1981, his papers

confiscated and his church ransacked, it was Jakov aged ten who came to the microphone in the church that evening to speak to the weeping people there; they had seen the children disappear suddenly to the room where Mary came to them. Jakov, made visible only by standing on the altar, explained that she was awaiting them there to tell them not to be afraid, that she wanted them to be happy and that she would look after Father Jozo.

Perhaps it was this which gave Jakov the idea that with the Virgin to teach him, school was superfluous; so in the autumn of 1981 he stayed at home. His cousin Mirjana is reported to have been asked by Mary to persuade him to return. He is now an orphan, his mother having died in 1983 when he was twelve and his father, a migrant worker, in May 1986. But it was before this, and soon after the visions began, that Vicka clearly heard the Virgin say to her, "Stay here with Jakov", and she gladly abandoned another attempt at the mathematics examination to do so. Jakov now lives with an aunt.

Though still uncertain of his future plans Jakov was in no doubt, when Mary spoke to them all of this in 1981, that he wished to join a monastery when he grew up; or in September 1985 that he intended to become a Franciscan friar; but he was to suffer a change of heart later that year as a consequence of Bishop Zanic's determination to bring about the downfall of Tomislav Vlasic.

Having already accused this priest of perjury and deception (pages 56–58) the bishop now charged him with the paternity of a nun's child, asking him to confess that "the Virgin is not appearing and that the whole business was your idea in the first place". Tomislav denied the charge under oath, protesting that the Virgin *is* appearing, so how could he possibly say that she is not? The charge was denied with equal vehemence by the ex-nun, who wrote to the bishop, "I have never revealed to anyone the name of my child's father." This deliberate defamation of the unhappy Tomislav was compounded by letters he had sent this woman as her adviser, offering spiritual comfort from information no doubt received in the confessional and therefore sacrosanct, so that he was unable to defend himself. The letters had clearly been stolen and their contents misrepresented; they were published in the U.S.A. by an able ally of the bishop's, Michael E. Jones, in a defamatory work entitled *Medjugorje: The Untold Story*.

That this nun became pregnant and bore a child is beyond doubt. That Vlasic was involved in any capacity other than as the nun's spiritual director is unlikely and unproven. Michael Jones quotes from letters alleged to have been written by the nun to Vlasic. If he returned these letters to her he was either innocent or a fool: yet his open countenance and the record of his ministry proclaim his integrity and deny the possibility of such stupidity.

Jakov, Ivan and Marija, with two friars and a nun, were summoned to Mostar in November 1985 to be informed by the bishop that in 1977 Father Tomislav had been responsible for the pregnancy of a certain nun who had recently emigrated to America. The shock and embarrassment of all present were only exceeded by the misery and desolation of Jakov, whose hero Tomislav was: still aged only fourteen, he wept bitterly; and though this scandal announced to the world was later proved slanderous, from that day Jakov gave up any idea of becoming a Franciscan priest.

He may adopt a locksmith's career, but meanwhile works in the parish bookshop. He is faithful in prayer, finding daily Holy Communion to be the centre of his life; and he still meets Mary daily, loving her as a Mother and as a good friend.

He is quick-witted in parrying all attempts to extract from him any secrets – he has travelled in Austria and Italy – and it seems possible that his year of military service may be as beneficial in maturity as it was for Ivan.

In nine years each of these six young people have grown in wisdom and in confident obedience to Mary's wish that they should perform the particular role which they believe that she, as God's messenger, is asking of them. They have seen the obscure village in which they were born and bred transformed into a place where almost every known language is heard, and where new buildings rise on all sides. Their families' means of livelihood has changed unrecognizably, as they devote their time and strength to being innkeepers for Mary's constantly arriving guests from every country in the world: and they still experience the joy and peace which Slavko decided, in 1982, could not be drug-induced.

SCIENCE

7
The Medical Teams

During the time that they say the Virgin is appearing
to them, the Six are thought by medical specialists as
well as certain theologians to be in a state of mystical
ecstasy, though they themselves make no such claim,
merely saying, "We see the Mother of God" (or *Gospa*).

From his specialized study of the subject, the Italian
Professor Margnelli recognized two forms of ecstasy:
that of a person who was unaware of their
surroundings, becoming rigid or even cataleptic; and
one who remained aware of the world and spoke as
an intermediary both to the people present as well as
to the unseen divine presence – a state which
describes the children's behaviour during the first
week. But when the initial excitement of conveying
Mary's response to the pleas or questions of the
assembled crowd had settled into a perception of what
she was conveying to each one of them, Margnelli
noted a third form of ecstasy. He defined this in 1985
as invincible and spontaneous – a state in which the
person is temporarily insensitive to anything but the
apparition on which their eyes are fixed, yet who is

socially well integrated and in a condition of perfectly normal mental and physical health.

It seems that the Medjugorje Six provide the first opportunity in history for reported visions to be observed, photographed, videoed and studied. Whatever may ultimately be proved or disproved, the first essential was an analysis of the children's state of mind and body, particularly during Mary's reported presence with them. This has been an ongoing task undertaken from day four by at least twenty-six medical doctors of both sexes specializing in psychology, psychiatry, neurology of various kinds and hypnotherapy, apart from bodily conditions of heart, sight, hearing, voice, brain and sensitivity to pain.

Laurentin saw a certain urgency in such an analysis, since Mary is quoted as saying that these are her last appearances on earth, one possible interpretation being that it is the last *before* some earth-shattering event. In either case, this may therefore be the last chance to acquire such knowledge.

Scientific tests cannot, however, establish what, if anything, is the object of the children's concentrated gaze or preclude its possible existence. Science has no complete explanation of ecstasy.

On day six the children were pronounced fit by a psychiatrist in Mostar, the nearest city. Then Dr Ludvik Stopar, director of a clinic in Maribor, Yugoslavia and a specialist in psychiatry and parapsychology, examined them in Medjugorje on four separate occasions, each of several days, between May 1982 and November 1983. Particularly interested

Fig. 1 Fr Jozo Zovko: the friar who saw The Madonna
Credit: Andre Durand

Fig. 2 Early days: the six see Mary. From left, Vicka, Jakov, Ivanka, Mirjana, Maria, Ivan

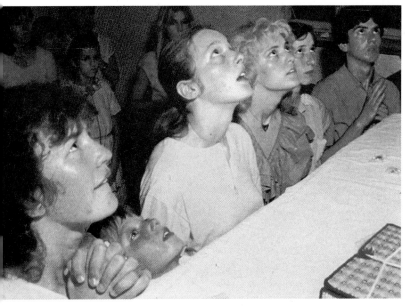

Fig. 3 The Church seen from the fields   Fig. 4 Podbrdo hill
Credit: Pat O'Sullivan   Credit: Clive Goble

Fig. 5 Podbrdo hill at dawn
Credit: Pat O'Sullivan

Fig. 6 Vicka today
Credit: Pat O'Sullivan

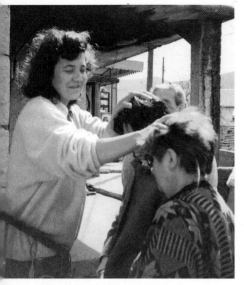

Fig. 7 Vicka outside her house
Credit: Pat O'Sullivan

Fig. 8 Jelena today
Credit: Pat O'Sullivan

Fig. 9 Confessionals at dawn, untypically empty
Credit: Clive Goble

Fig. 10 Confessionals in typical use
Credit: Clive Goble

Fig. 11 The climb to Krizevac
Credit: Clive Goble

Fig. 12 Krizevac at dawn
Credit: Clive Goble

Fig. 14 Krizevac Cross with lightning
conductor
Credit: Clive Goble

Fig. 13 Krizevac: last station of the
Cross — The Resurrection
Credit: Clive Goble

Fig. 15 Church entrance at dawn
Credit: Clive Goble

Fig. 16 Church interior at dawn, untypically empty
Credit: Clive Goble

Fig. 17 Church interior typically crowded
Credit: Clive Goble

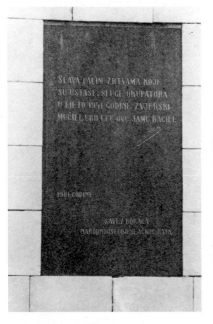

Fig. 18 Surmanci column inscription
Credit: Clive Goble

Fig. 19 Surmanci pit, flags and column
Credit: Clive Goble

Fig. 20 Surmanci pit after December 1990
Credit: Clive Goble

in these events which had taken place in his own country, his aim was to make a statement of the facts for Bishop Zanic's first commission of inquiry (page 59) and though his approach was theological he found that the police respected his freedom to undertake scientific research.

As the first doctor to have made a methodical investigation of the children during ecstasy, he found them to be normal: when they believed themselves to be speaking naturally their lips were in fact moving silently (as was the case with Bernadette)[1] and Marija continued to see the vision when he stood in front of her, saying afterwards that she had only noticed a light haze.

He chose Marija, whom he thought the most intelligent and mature, as a subject for hypnosis, the means by which he believed it possible to isolate the 90 per cent conscious level of the mind in order to detect possible manipulation. Having already asked her to tell him about the visions, she repeated the account to him for an hour while hypnotized, the only variation being that whereas she had previously guarded the secrets with much care, under hypnosis she disclosed them. Marija was aware only of the unconscious 10 per cent, apologizing to the doctor for having fallen asleep during his interview. Stopar assured the shocked Laurentin that the secrets were as safe with him as with Marija and that he would regard them as though heard in the confessional; and further that he considered himself justified

1 *Mother of Nations*, p. 96.

therapeutically in failing to ask Marija's permission, feeling sure that she would have refused it.

His impression was that he had been in contact with a supernatural reality; and he requested that a canonical process should examine objectively and establish rigorously that ''these psychological phenomena are theist and transcendent; that they are not the result of human manipulation''.

The location of the Virgin's daily appearances has changed several times, firstly from the hill due to police intervention, then from various other places which were in turn forbidden by the bishop presumably because he hoped that by frustrating the crowds of attendant pilgrims the children and friars would admit defeat. But the children have not stopped claiming that the Virgin appears to them daily, and until April 1985 she came to a previously disused chapel in the church to the right of the sanctuary. It was there that Dr Stopar was with them, and there that they were seen by teams of Italian and French doctors in 1983–4.

Henri Joyeux, a professor in the Medical Faculty of Montpellier, Paris, told a reporter that he was interested in all phenomena which science finds inexplicable. He had read Father Laurentin's first book about Medjugorje (it had also influenced Wayne Weible among many others) and he brought to Medjugorje a team of four medical specialists, and a technician to monitor the electrical equipment it had been decided to use. Laurentin worked with them during their visits of several days in March, June, October and December 1984. All went well until June, when they prepared to connect the electrical apparatus to the visionaries' heads, and when Jakov demonstrated the children's rapport with Mary by saying that the Virgin had told them it was not necessary. It says something for the reality of this uniquely extraordinary situation that these six learned men awaited Mary's answer through young Jakov, the spokesman, with considerable anxiety.

Jakov was asked to tell her that just as the promised Sign would be useful for non-believers, so would their scientific tests; and after that evening's ecstasy it was with vast relief that they received Mary's answer through Jakov: "You did well to ask. You can go ahead." These tests were not made in the chapel to the right of the sanctuary, but in the sacristy to the left, where the necessary electric sockets existed.

The medical and theological experts seem agreed on the significance of the synchronization with which the visionaries react while in ecstasy. Their daily appointment with Mary is kept at 6.40 p.m. in summer and at 5.40 in winter. At the agreed place they stand in line facing a wall on which hangs a crucifix and begin to say the Lord's prayer, together and aloud, before kneeling suddenly and *in perfect unison*. The wall has disappeared in a blaze of light. Standing on a cloud in the midst of this great light is the smiling *Gospa*, their rapt faces and silently moving lips the only evidence of her presence. They are suddenly silent *as one*, having reached "Who art in heaven": Mary has taken up the prayer and is saying it with them. Then there is a pause during which they appear to be speaking inaudibly, as though seen through a window. All eyes are concentrated on or near the crucifix still visible to everyone but themselves, while they listen and respond to Mary's messages. Their voices then resume *as one* after "Our Father . . .": Mary has begun the prayer. Finally they raise their heads and eyes as one before saying "*Ode*" (she has gone). Mary has returned to heaven or, as they put it, disappeared upwards.

All this is regarded as proof at least of objectivity, since there is clearly no collusion or prearranged signal. Can one assume that they are seeing and communicating with an object or person which science cannot identify and which is invisible to all but themselves; and with which, furthermore, they are on easy if not filial terms?

Elaborate tests were made before, during and after the ecstasy. Those of the Italians had shown the Six to be leading perfectly normal lives, and to have lucid recall of all that had happened; and they eliminated any suspicion of neurosis, epilepsy, catalepsy, hysteria, hallucination or drug-taking, findings which the French team confirmed. In addition, by their use of an electroencephalogram, states of sleep, dream and mass hallucination were also ruled out by the French. They measured alpha-beta brain rhythms, alpha indicating wakeful receptivity – the state, for example, of the contemplative in prayer, and beta signifying the rhythm of discussion and activity. It was found that when the visionaries awaited Mary their beta or activity rhythm changed to an almost continuous alpha, believed to be that of contemplatives and mystics, as well as of drivers on long journeys. This is a rather complicated way of proving that they are still and attentive, at least for the limited time of the visionary presence.

Other instruments checked the normality of heart-beat, sight, hearing and voice-production. Light flashed in their eyes by an electro-oculogram during ecstasy caused no blinking or other reaction; Ivan was unaware of a sudden loud noise by his ear; and a screen in front of them no more obscured the vision than had Dr Stopar's large figure. They were also shown to be impervious to pain during ecstasy, proved by an algometer and by the medieval test for ecstasy performed on the unsuspecting Vicka, who failed to react to a needle (unsterilized) plunged twice into her shoulder from behind. She was later surprised when shown the bloodstained evidence on her sleeve.

Tests undertaken by these highly qualified "foreign doctors" were dismissed by members of the bishop's second Commission on grounds of their ignorance of the language of the country; a sad comment on that country's interpreters and on its own Dr Stopar, whose request for an unbiased canonical examination the Commission seem to have disregarded. They may also have overlooked the fact that anyone in Communist Yugoslavia who was known to be associated with Medjugorje at that time would have been suspect.

Dr Stopar excluded the possibility of the visionaries being mediums; and Laurentin points out that they are not taken over by a different personality, but are always aware of their identity. He too considers the hypothesis of mediumship a false trail.

When Vicka was too ill to leave her house Joyeux filmed her at home during a vision. By a comparison

of her own calm manner and transfigured face with
the behaviour of someone who knelt beside her, he
was able to illustrate the agitation, excitement and
exaggerated gestures of a pathological as opposed to
a genuine ecstatic.

Professor Margnelli, the specialist in ecstasy, (page
95) makes another comparison. The visionaries in
ecstasy are insensitive to everything but the vision on
which their whole attention is concentrated, so that
attempts to distract them by sight, sound or touch are
like telephoning an empty house. There is no answer
because the family are in another place. ''The
telephone, metaphorically speaking, had rung on a
spirit that was somewhere else'', conclusions reached
by Dr Margnelli, a scientist who went to Medjugorje
in 1985 a critical atheist and is now a Christian.

The Six can never calculate the duration of a vision,
whether it was of one minute or forty-five, but each
occasion brings them joyous expectation and much
happiness. On day five they asked Mary why she
didn't appear in the church so that everybody could
see her, to be told, ''Happy are those who have not
seen and yet believe'',[2] Christ's words to doubting
Thomas.

Is this a mystery outside time and space, and at
present incapable even of scientific verification?

2 St John 20:29.

8
Ionizing Radiation

There was a flurry of excitement in 1987 when measurements taken in Medjugorje with an electroscope were published; but claims of scientific proof for the existence of the spiritual world seem to have proved short-lived.

Since March 1985 Dr B. Lipinski of The Foundation for the Study of Bio-electricity in Boston, U.S.A. and Professor E. Mor, a professor of Electro-chemistry at Genoa University, have conducted and compared some very interesting investigations at Medjugorje, using an electroscope to measure comparative radiation; for example on the hill of apparitions, in the church during Holy Communion, and in the room of apparitions one Friday.

A reading was taken which Lipinski considered tentatively to be so high as to be either dangerous, as at Chernobyl, or alternatively of spiritual rather than of nuclear origin; while Professor Mor was of the opinion that the concentration had no logical explanation, asking, ''Where is this radiation coming from?'' Dr Lipinski concludes that since similar energy is not generated in churches or in crowded sports gatherings, it may be associated with intensity and quality of prayer, combined with the fasting which is practised in Medjugorje every Friday; though the highest reading was that taken in the room of apparitions.

Dr T. W. Alexander, a consultant radiologist in Durham, England observes, in a letter of August 1990 to the author, that there are many sophisticated machines available which can analyse radiation and thereby indicate its possible origin; but he points out that the device used by Dr Lipinski (an electroscope) is too primitive to provide information as to the nature of any radiation it may detect. It may be compared to an instrument that can detect sound, but will not be able to distinguish between the noise of thunder and that of a barking dog. Its lack of precision would make it hard to exclude a simple machine fault as the cause of its intermittently high readings. He adds that Professor Mor notes the presence of numbers of electrically charged particles such as exist in thunderstorms, though without defining their possible significance to the reports of the visionaries.

Investigations of radioactivity in Medjugorje have been conducted by other scientists who have not, however, made the same deductions regarding the presence of spiritual energy.

Yet Lipinski may have tiptoed into a realm of potentially tremendous and awe-inspiring importance and deserving of continuing research; so it is disappointing to learn that when, a year later in 1986 he was prepared for further study, the Yugoslavian airport authorities considered his technical equipment to be so dangerously suspicious as to refuse him entry for a further two years. No more has as yet been heard of his researches, though Laurentin commented in 1988 that Dr Lipinski was not able to verify his suppositions.

Laurentin noted in 1987 that the visions cannot be explained by ionization, or by other radiations, nor by a magnetic field. Dr Lipinski's hypothesis, on the other hand, seemed to be that it was the visions which were the cause *and* effect of the quite abnormally high reading of 100,000 millirads per hour of the ionizing radiation in the visionary room, compared to 500 on Podbrdo.

But if *natural* or *scientific* explanations of the visions are to be excluded, can it be deduced that they are of *supernatural* origin; or that they exist only in the imagination of the Six?

Gitta Sereny notes that Professor Bélanger,[1] Sivric's editor and collaborator (page 63) considers the possibility of geophysical forces releasing electromagnetic effects which could affect the brain and create hallucinations, the character of which would depend on the cultural background of the subject, for example, a child who had been taught Christianity. Thus Bélanger writes that the children of Medjugorje have seen a luminous phenomenon which they have interpreted, according to their culture, as being the Virgin Mary or the *Gospa*; but it has to be said that a good many other people have seen luminous

1 See bibliography.

phenomena at Medjugorje, not all of which they have been able to identify as the *Gospa*. Equally, no natural or scientific solution has yet been suggested to account for the phenomenon of the sun appearing to spin while surrounded by whirling multi-colours. A great many people either singly or in groups claim to have observed this, both in Medjugorje and at other Marian shrines, notably Walsingham, England, Fatima, Portugal and Oliveto Citra, Italy. At Fatima on 13 October 1917 the same phenomenon was experienced by thousands of people, most of whom thought it signalled the end of the world. Known as the Miracle of the Sun it was regarded, at least by the Catholic Church, as proof of the sixth and last of the Virgin Mary's appearances there (*Mother of Nations* page 39).

A possible effect of the presence of spiritual energy in Medjugorje concerns the metal of rosaries, a rosary being a string or chain circlet of beads on which prayers are counted.

It is an undoubted fact that since about 1986 the chain links of many rosaries acquired at or taken to Medjugorje have changed in appearance from silver to gold. By July 1991 no scientific explanation had been offered, and whether golden rosaries were a myth or a mystery was still being debated. There are accounts of a metal chain on which only some of the links turned gold in colour; and of a man who left Medjugorje with a normal rosary of silver-coloured links and on arrival in Rome found that it had become golden. Bill Reck of the Riehle Foundation (see ''Eight Years'' by Laurentin) has received hundreds of reports of these phenomena.

A professional collector of coins explained that constant use with sweaty hands would remove the very thin layer of silver, exposing the underlying brass of the chain; but he did not say why this should occur only in Medjugorje, and not with rosaries put to equally hard use in such warm climates as France and Portugal.

Robert Brophy[2], who wrote that he had spent many years testing metals professionally, reported of a Medjugorje rosary he was asked to examine that whereas he expected to find that the surface only had changed, the gold colour had in fact fused through the links, making them a different metal. He discounted forgery.

A Jesuit priest[3] climbing Krizevac and cracking jokes with a friend about the chances of the coins in their pockets turning to gold may have stopped laughing when he *saw* the rosary in his hand turn gold in colour. In 1988, another priest[4], who was rather afraid the whole affair might be of the devil, prayed about it in Medjugorje where he was reminded of Wisdom 3:6. "God has put them to the test and proved them worthy to be with him; he has tested them like gold in a furnace, and accepted them . . ." Back in the U.S.A. and *before* he began to write up what he regarded as a clear and conclusive explanation, his own rosaries had become golden.

What seems incapable of scientific proof, nor to be

2 *Medjugorje Messenger* No. 17 of 1990.
3 *Tablet* p. 671 for 26 May 1990.
4 *Medjugorje Messenger* No. 11 for September 1988.

accounted for by any early cultural influence, is the story of a certain Russian scientist called Sarej Grib who found his way to Medjugorje in 1989. Educated by atheists he went on to learn physics at Leningrad University, specializing in the study of atmospheric phenomena and earth magnetic fields. He considers his present faith as an Eastern Orthodox Christian to be a miracle, since all his early training taught him to deny the existence of God.

While still at school he had a vivid dream, the reality of which persists and has affected his entire life. The dream was of an icon or picture of Mary, the light from which seemed to illuminate his soul and fill him with peace and an inexpressible joy, enabling him to encounter God. Although he could not convey to his sceptical parents the reason for his changed attitude to life, he was much helped by a *staretz* or traditional Russian counsellor, who convinced him without words of the truth of Christianity. He now belongs to an association in Leningrad which deals with problems of science and faith. Later on, like Wayne Weible, he watched a video of Medjugorje, but with a friend who was a professor of biology with whom he talked it over. The friend became a priest and he himself, by then a married man with children, was persuaded by a Cardinal to go to Medjugorje. He was present there for the eighth anniversary of the visions, when he is quoted as saying, ''I seem to find here the answer to all world questions.''

It is as necessary to beware the pitfalls of leaping to false conclusions, of uncritical enthusiasm or of bending the facts to fit the fiction, as of the bias of total disbelief. In the opinion of the publisher[5] Bill Reck, a simple solution of the conundrum of the golden rosaries is to say that there has never been any acceptable explanation but the obvious one. Let Gamaliel[6] have the last word: "If this enterprise. . .is of human origin it will break up of its own accord; but if it does in fact come from God. . .you might find yourselves fighting against God."

5 Riehle Foundation, Ohio.
6 Acts of the Apostles 5:38.

HISTORY

9
Bitter Conflict

In offering an objective view of these events in Medjugorje it is relevant and even necessary briefly to touch on the very complex historical background of the country in which they occurred.

The kingdom of the Serbs, Croats and Slovenes which became part of Yugoslavia in 1929, has a long history of invasion and oppression.

Of the six republics which compose Yugoslavia, the Christians of Slovenia, Croatia and Bosnia-Hercegovina have been mainly Roman Catholic since the seventh century, while Serbia, Montenegro and Macedonia had become Eastern Orthodox by 981. Croatia and Serbia may be said to epitomize the racial and religious strife which has characterized the country since the ninth century, and still (1991) dominates its present democratically elected government.

The Serbs and Croats were Southern Slavs from Asia, who had settled in the Balkans by the fifth century A.D. Although they spoke the same language as each other, they were influenced by the decision of 395 A.D. which divided the Roman Empire's rule between Constantinople in the East and Rome in the West. From the different interpretations of the Christian Gospel implied by this division, and by their geographical location, the Serbs gave their allegiance to the Eastern Orthodox Church and the Croats to the Roman Catholic. Opposed to both these versions of Christianity were the Bogomils, a dualist religious sect founded by a priest of that name, who reached Yugoslavia from Bulgaria in the eleventh century.

By the end of the twelfth century the Eastern Church had driven the heretical Bogomils out of Serbia. They then fled to Bosnia where, by the early thirteenth century, they regarded themselves as Christians of the Bosnian Church.

The missionary followers of St Francis of Assisi (d. 1226) began to preach the Gospel to Bosnia in 1339, consolidating their position by converting the Bogomil king to Latin Christianity; and within four years they had founded thirty-six monasteries in the district.

Since there were few secular clergy, by 1378 the Pope gave Franciscans the right to become priests and to build churches, with the particular trust of converting the Bogomils to Roman Catholicism. The Franciscans gradually became responsible for the spiritual welfare of both Bosnia and Hercegovina and the original foreign Franciscan missionaries soon inspired members of their flock to join them, thus initiating the long history of pastoral care which survived the Turkish persecution, ultimately resulting in the Hercegovnia Case described in chapter four.

The Turks had adopted the faith of Islam in the seventh century, Mohammed having died in 652. Their

Ottoman Empire had by 1354 overrun Asia Minor, conquering the Balkans in 1480.

They overcame Serbia in 1459, when large numbers of Serbian Orthodox Christians fled north to the predominantly Catholic Croatia and Bosnia, from which time on Yugoslavian Christians of East and West have found some difficulty in accepting each other's religious differences. By 1483 the north, too, had fallen to the Turks.

Though of the same Slavic origin Croats and Serbs became mortally opposed to each other, an enmity exacerbated by their divergent understanding of Christianity as represented by Western Roman Catholicism and Eastern Orthodoxy. Embers of this fire of opposition were to smoulder until they burst into flames in the present century, a conflagration in which the area of Medjugorje was crucially involved.

10
The Turks Take Over

The Ottoman Turks occupied what is now Yugoslavia from 1478 to 1878.

During these four hundred years and after the secular clergy had fled from the invading Turks, the Croat Franciscan friars of Bosnia and Hercegovina stood firm. By putting off their brown religious habits and growing Turkish style drooping moustaches, they sought to avoid identification by the pursuing Moslems, staying with the people and continuing to administer Holy Communion and to baptize, marry and bury them.

They thus formed such close ties and so long a memory of sharing the lives and religious persecution of these people, of whom they were a part, that as their priests and bishops they became, and to a great extent still are, as one family. A man who farmed grapes and tobacco near Medjugorje told Robert Faricy in 1985 "The priest was our brother, who laughed with us and wept with us: he was one of us"[4] –

1 *Medjugorje Unfolds*, 46, Faricy (see bibliography).

a man who may be said to speak for the great majority.

This sense of mutual trust and understanding between priests and people, who shared their faith in God in this isolated corner of Christendom, has persisted to the present day and is undoubtedly a factor in the Franciscan presence in Medjugorje. It may even be relevant to the alleged appearances of the Mother of God in that particular part of the world.

In Yugoslavia, according to Laurentin, Serbian Orthodox believers considerably outnumber Roman Catholics. But since these alleged appearances from 24 June 1981 occurred in a village whose pastors were Franciscan friars in a predominantly Roman Catholic part of the country, it is the fortunes of that Croat region which are most relevant here.

During the reign of Stephen II, a fourteenth-century Bogomil king of Bosnia, Hercegovina (meaning the Dukedom) became part of his kingdom. But the Bogomils gradually disappeared, their only monument the carved tombstones, some near Medjugorje, inscribed in the Cyrillic script which was brought to the Balkans from Constantinople by the ninth-century brothers Saints Cyril and Methodius, the "Apostles of the Slavs". Cyrillic script is still used in the liturgy of the Serbian Orthodox Church; but the Bogomil *stecci* or tombstones are perhaps a symbol and foreboding of the religious strife which has since then characterized Yugoslav history.

After the Turkish conquest the Bogomil landowners of Bosnia found that their future security lay with Islam. Once they had understood that by becoming

Moslems they would be exempt from taxes and permitted to retain their noble rank, possessions and land, their conversion to Islam seemed to them a small price to pay for these privileges. Keeping their feudal rights and Slavic language, their life style remained essentially the same, though outwardly they became indistinguishable from Moslems in their dress and behaviour and soon came to be regarded as Turks. The Christians paid heavy taxes and incurred severe penalties, some being enslaved by their Bogomil-turned-Moslem landlords.

The Turks persecuted, hunted and killed those who were non-Moslems, treating any remaining Christian priests – by definition friars – with particular harshness.

Bosnia and Hercegovina became a Turkish province and Moslem stronghold in 1463, one effect of which was probably to strengthen the racial and religious awareness of those who remained Christian against considerable odds. The Serbs, on the other hand, having had their country annexed by Turkey in 1459, were able to treat the Turks as occupying invaders only.

The Franciscan monasteries were destroyed and the friars dispersed, ministering to the people in secret, who in turn protected them treating them as ''Uncles''; but if, as often happened, the friars were caught they were tortured and killed. With their followers, many of them took to the mountains of Hercegovina and the Adriatic coast, sharing the lives of their people and at one with them. They acted as teachers and medical doctors, as well as priests and bishops – a proud heritage for these undoubtedly humble disciples of Christ and St Francis.

It was they who preserved Christianity in Bosnia and Hercegovina, despite the centuries-long and relentless attempts on the part of their Turkish Moslem rulers to eradicate it.

After its defeat at Vienna in 1683 the power of the Ottoman Empire began to decline; and in 1878 at the Berlin Congress, the boundaries of the Balkan states were settled and the Turkish occupation ended. Bosnia-Hercegovina was then administered (or occupied) by Austro-Hungary.

The religious adherence of the present population of the regions of Bosnia-Hercegovina and Croatia where the visions are said to be occurring – that is to say Sarajevo, Mostar and Medjugorje – is equally distributed between Eastern Orthodox, Roman Catholic and Moslem, a distribution referred to on page 31, and relevant to certain messages which the Six claim to have received from the Virgin.

11
Marshal Tito

The mountains of Hercegovina and Dalmatia, which had provided sanctuary for Christians during four hundred years of Turkish occupation, were also to provide hide-outs for Tito's Partisans during the German occupation of 1941-5.

It was the concerted efforts of the Southern Slavs which finally ousted the Turks when for a time peace and unity between Serb and Croat seemed possible. But when the Turkish domination ended in 1878 Bosnia-Hercegovina was occupied by Austro-Hungary, who annexed it in 1908. Racial and religious strife between Serb and Croat was perpetuated, since a united nation was seen as a threat to the territorial ambition of their new masters, the kings of Austria and Hungary, who therefore encouraged the old mistrust, hatred and dissension: a policy which led to something far worse than their own downfall.

The identification of nationality with religious allegiance has always been characteristic of Yugoslavia, where to be Croat is to be Roman Catholic and to be Serb, Orthodox. The Slav Moslems, too, were officially recognized in 1918 as a separate nation, though they lived predominantly in Bosnia-Hercegovina and were of course the descendants of those Slavs who had accepted Turkish protection in the fifteenth century.

The annexation of their country by Austro-Hungary was particularly resented by Serbia, opposition which found expression on 28 June 1914 in Sarajevo (capital of Bosnia-Hercegovina and home of Mirjana) where a Serb nationalist assassinated the visiting Archduke of Austria. He was heir to the Dual Monarchy, causing Austro-Hungary to declare war on Serbia and precipitating the outbreak of the First World War.

Hope of Southern Slavic peace and unity was revived at the end of that war by the creation of a new kingdom of Serbs, Croats and Slovenes; and in a dictatorship proclaimed in 1929 King Alexander, a Serb, renamed the country Yugoslavia – the land of the Southern Slavs. But royalist Chetnik Serbs, or freedom fighters, were opposed by the Croat Ustasa,[1] a rebel, nationalist and anti-Communist organization; and during a state visit to France in 1934 the king was in turn assassinated by an Ustasa representative.

As exiled leader of the outlawed Ustase, Ante Pavelic then became a key figure. Motivated by bitter hatred of Serbia and the Orthodox Church, his adherents were trained in Italy and Hungary by Mussolini's Fascists, with the object of establishing an independent Catholic Croatia in opposition to Eastern Orthodox Serbia.

In touch with the Germans, Pavelic returned from

1 Ustasa is singular, Ustase plural.

Italy in April 1941, when Croatia was divided laterally between Italy and Germany. The Independent State of Croatia – known as NDH from its Yugoslav name of Nezavisna Drzava Hrvatska – had been proclaimed in Zagreb, the capital, five days before his arrival, by his henchman in command of the underground Ustasa army, with Nazi approval and backing.

The Ustasa Party now ruled the NDH, which was led by Pavelic. The European war of 1939-45 had provided the opportunity for which he had been waiting; and having declared their devotion to the Catholic Church, the NDH made an immediate decision that the religion of the new state should be Catholic and Moslem only, use of the words "Serbian Orthodox religion" being forbidden.

The royalist Chetniks had long been engaged in ruthless guerilla warfare against the Croats when Yugoslavia was invaded in 1941. They then continued to massacre the Croats and in addition took on the Germans, Ustase and Communists; and if accounts of the tactics adopted by the Ustase make the blood run cold, those of the Chetniks may well have inspired them – for example, in the matter of throwing people alive into pits and burying them.

The chief aim and purpose of the Ustasa government appears to have been the defeat of the royalist Chetniks, with the general object not merely of subjugating those Serbs who were domiciled in Croatia, but of eliminating those they could neither convert to Catholicism nor deport.

In an edict issued by the Minister of Education, Mile Budak, one third were to be deported, one third (the educated) killed and one third (the uneducated) converted to Catholicism. The Croat Moslems, on the other hand, were to be treated as brothers and allies. *On 24 June 1941*, exactly forty years before the Six say that the Virgin Mary appeared to them, the edict was put into effect by an organization called the State Directorate for Renewal, which set up camps as assembly points.

A good deal of light was thrown on the implementation of Budak's edict by German Security Police Reports, such as:

> The atrocities perpetrated by the Ustase units against the Orthodox in Croatian territory must be regarded as the most important reason for the blazing up of guerilla activities. The Ustase units have carried out their atrocities not only against male Orthodox of military age, but in particular in the most bestial fashion against unarmed old men, women and children . . .(17 February 42)

and in the same report

> The number of Orthodox who have been butchered and tortured to death by the most sadistic methods must number an estimated 300,000 persons.[2]

Well before the claimed visions of June 1981, Trevor Beeson wrote: ''It is impossible to understand the present religious situation in Yugoslavia without taking

2 See Stella Alexander (bibliography) pp. 23 and 29.

account of the wartime sufferings of the country, and in particular of the Orthodox Christians.''[3] Their sufferings are a crucial part of the recent history of Croatia, and cannot therefore be disregarded in any attempted objective appraisal of the events in Medjugorje.

One effect of these afflictions, not lost on the Germans, was that not only Serbs but also Croats fled to join Tito's resistance movement, which began arming and training in the mountains of Hercegovina from June 1941.

The Catholic Church hoped for many conversions but wanted only those who came of their own choice, no doubt remembering the Papal Bull of 1302 that ''it is altogether necessary for salvation for every creature to be subject to the Roman Pontiff''; whereas the Orthodox were sure that they had held ''right (Christian) belief, glory and worship'' since well before their schism with Rome in 1054.[4] The NDH, on the other hand, wanted the conversion of the uneducated; and on 30 July 1941 certain priests were required to assist them in the mass murder of Serbs disinclined for conversion, though some accepted Catholicism as the only means of avoiding slaughter.

As head of the Catholic Church in Croatia, Archbishop Stepinac knew of the existence of the Ustase, but it seemed that ''he had closed his eyes to the fact that behind them were the Italian Fascists and Nazi Germany''.[5] He was appalled when he realized

3 Beeson (bibliography) p. 306.
4 Ware (bibliography) pp. 16, 22.
5 Stella Alexander p. 149.

that some of his priests were implicated in these massacres. He was also deeply distressed by what he saw as Pavelic's Judas kiss and by the corruption of the NDH from which he had expected so much good. He protested privately to Pavelic in a letter, and from 1942 onwards he denounced the NDH publicly and preached against the persecution of Serbs.

The Orthodox Metropolitan (Archbishop) of Zagreb was arrested, severely beaten, and imprisoned after the proclamation of the NDH. Eventually expelled to Serbia, he died in 1945 from the effects of this ill-treatment. Amongst other such atrocities, a bishop in Croatia who refused to leave his diocese was moved to a concentration camp at Gospic where, with 2000 other Serbs, he was then taken to a ravine in the Velebit mountains, where all were killed.

There seems no doubt that certain Franciscan friars were members of the Ustasa and took part in these massacres. Certain others who had joined the Ustase before the war were described as unworthy men of narrow patriotism, whose novitiate in Siena was near Pavelic's headquarters. There they were influenced by ideas which, on their return to Yugoslavia, they passed on to pupils in Franciscan schools, in particular that at Siroki Brijeg which produced some influential Ustase leaders, and happens to be about 20 miles from Medjugorje. But it is also true to say that there were some Orthodox priests who fought with the Serb Chetniks and massacred Croats.

Archbishop Stepinac found himself in a position of spiritual anguish, since he longed for conversions to what he regarded as the true faith (the Unam Sanctum of 1302), yet shuddered from Ustase terrorism as a means to attain that end.

It seems clear that Pavelic's hatred of Serbs and the Christian church they represented led to his own eventual downfall and escape to Argentina in 1945. It was the determination of the Orthodox Chetniks and Catholic Ustase to destroy each other, with the same ultimate object of gaining power and post-war control of their country rather than of uniting for its peace, which enabled Tito's Communists to beat them.

It was Tito's organized opposition to the occupying Germans which, from January 1944, gained him the recognition and backing of the Allied armies previously given to the Chetniks; and in October 1944, by an agreement with Russia, his Partisan troops entered Belgrade with units of the Red Army. He became a Marshal and from November 1943 governed the country, uniting Yugoslavia's six nations as a Federal Republic in 1945.

This unity was not achieved, however, before the triumphant Partisans had committed atrocities which equalled if not excelled any that either Chetnik or Ustasa had thought of – such as surrounding the monastery of Siroki Brijeg and killing both the friars and any others who had sought sanctuary there.

President Tito had joined the Communist Party in 1920; but his independence of Soviet authority led to the expulsion of the Yugoslav Communist Party from Stalin's Cominform in 1948.

Tito's memory had been honoured annually since his death on 4 May 1980. But ten years later, in May 1990, a Serbian crowd in Belgrade was shouting anti-

Tito slogans and blaming Tito, a Croat, for the Communist Federation which deprived them of their monarchy; and in the same month the first free multi-party elections in Croatia and Slovenia voted decisively for *non-Communist* representation by the Croatian Democratic Union.

It seems that in August 1945 the Catholic Church thought that the Communist regime could not last. The bishops condemned atheism but rejoiced in ''the lively devotion to the Mother of God and the great number of pilgrimages to her shrines''. The annual procession to Maria Bistrica had not been forbidden.

In October of 1989 a gathering of Catholic and Orthodox Christians, Moslems and Jews met in Belgrade and agreed on a petition about religious freedom, which included a demand that the regulations requiring teachers to present Marxism as the only scientifically valid view of the world should be revoked: and in July 1990 the Catholic Archbishop of Belgrade spoke of being on good and friendly terms with the Serbian Orthodox Church hierarchy and believers.

Also in July 1990, in Slovenia and Croatia, mass graves were found, containing the remains of victims of the Partisans during and after the war. Branco Mulic, a former Communist, aged 80, who had been sworn to silence, felt freed by the May elections which had ended Communism to disclose to journalists the whereabouts of a thirty-foot deep pit (one of many) to which in 1945 he had driven a lorry containing fifty wounded Croats, whose execution he witnessed. A burial service for them conducted by Doctor Sustar,

Catholic Archbishop of Ljubljana, Slovenia was regarded as reflecting the Church's teaching on forgiveness, though this did not mean *forgetting* misdeeds. It was the parish priest who pointed out that these discoveries of Communist atrocities proved the falsity of their accusations against the Ustase and Chetniks as the only perpetrators of such terrorism.

Painful and divisive though these facts of Yugoslav history before, during and after the Second World War undoubtedly are, they must surely be remembered rather than forgotten, since otherwise they will continue to divide, bedevil and confuse this most courageous, independent and devout people whose very courage may account for their ruthlessness in the pursuit of what they saw, however blindly, as the right.

In the context of this history, and of the Ustase bands that took to the hills and woods in the autumn of 1945, the over-reaction of the atheist police in June 1981 is understandable (pages 25 and 28). They could hardly fail to be suspicious of huge crowds who assembled on a hillside – particularly *that* hill, for reasons which may be clear in the next chapter – in the cause of some alleged religious manifestation.

There had been an overwhelming response to the pilgrimage sanctioned in July 1945 to the shrine of Maria Bistrica, (page 127) when about 50,000 people found their way there on foot in the considerable heat of a Croatian summer. The Communists were startled, both by the numbers and the fact that the pilgrims represented families whose members had fled, disappeared or been killed.

The authorities were even more startled in 1984, when an estimated throng of 300,000 people turned up there to celebrate three hundred years of the shrine's existence; an orderly and happy crowd, which made no political demonstrations. Peace and forgiveness seem to have been in the air that day. The Serbian Orthodox Patriarch was present, besides representatives of the Government and of other religious communities including Moslems. A few days earlier the Patriarch had consecrated a church built on the site of the dreaded Ustase concentration camp at Jasenovac, in which thousands of Serbs, Croats and Jews had died.

Croatian devotion to Mary the Mother of God has a long history, and was commended by the Pope in 1979, when he welcomed 10,000 Croat pilgrims to Rome. There they heard Mass celebrated in St Peter's for the first time ever in their own language.

At an international conference at Ampleforth Abbey in Yorkshire, England in August 1990 about the failure of Communism, Archbishop Sustar spoke of the reawakening of Christianity and the longing, especially among the young, for transcendence – for genuine values for living, for definite moral rules and for a final meaning to life; words which seem to paraphrase and even interpret Mary's gentle and persistent message to the thousands of young pilgrims who flock constantly to Medjugorje.

Her requests there have been for peace, forgiveness and repentance for sin (or regret for errors). She first appeared, it is said, a little over a year after Tito's death, when the country was in a condition of turmoil and uncertainty, and the police were particularly wary of any signs of a resurgence of religious activity or of the strife they associated with it. But they have found nothing to fear from Medjugorje, which brings only orderly crowds and a great deal of hard currency; and that there Mary is venerated by Catholic, Orthodox, Moslem and even Communist, and that they all seek her protection and prayers.

By 1990 it seemed possible that Tito's federation might be replaced by a confederation, which would eventually satisfy all the republics and bring peace and independence to the still warring Serbs and Croats.

Meanwhile nationalist demonstrations and violence have escalated since Croatia, Slovenia and Bosnia-Hercegovina rejected Communist rule.

12
Surmanci

One name that is likely to be remembered rather than forgotten, in the context of the many fearful memories and events of the NDH reign of terror, is Glina — symbol and memorial of shame to Croatia and suffering to Serbia. It was in the village of Glina in May 1941 that the Ustase rounded up the 1500 male Serbian inhabitants (which presumably included boy children) and packed them into the village church. There they were not, as they had anticipated, converted to Catholicism, but hacked to death. But it has to be said that there were Serbian repercussions; and that in April 1941 the Chetniks destroyed two Croatian villages and massacred their inhabitants.

On a hill outside Mostar there is a well-kept war graves cemetery of the honoured Partisans, who died "contributing to the national liberation struggle". Near Medjugorje two less conspicuous memorials commemorate the deaths, in 1941, of certain other people.

Five or six miles from Medjugorje, in the scenically beautiful valley of the Neretva river, the Serbian

Orthodox monastery of Zitomislic was built in the late
sixteenth century. Very little is now left of the original
buildings, which continued to be inhabited by monks
until *21 June 1941*. On that day the Ustase broke into
and burned down the monastery, having first seized
the monks, whom they then took across the river
before burying them alive.

The monastery was rebuilt and is now a convent of
nuns, a fresco of the Annunciation above the door of
their new church being the only treasure preserved
from the destruction.

In November 1989 a Catholic priest led a party of four
people – two Anglicans, two Croatians – to the
convent, where a weeping nun pointed to a plaque on
the wall at the right of the church door. The plaque,
put there on *21 June 1981*, records those terrible deaths
forty years before, with the names of the entire
community of fifteen monks who died, and whose
death was commemorated exactly three days before
six children in Medjugorje quietly insisted that the
Mother of God had appeared and spoken to them.

In 1941, of five small villages encircling a fertile plain
at the foot of the mountains in Hercegovina,
Medjugorje was distinguishable only by its church; the
other hamlets were Bijakovici, nearest to Medjugorje;
Miletina, Vionica, and Surmanci, where there is only
a small chapel and some scattered farms.

Near this chapel there is an inconspicuous path
leading to a steep and stony ravine at the foot of the
hill. On the edge of the ravine stands a four-sided
concrete column with an inscription, and some ten to
twelve feet below the column there is a circular space

with a concrete surface six or more yards across. This surface conceals a deep pit in the natural rock.

On 6 August 1941 a train on the Mostar to Capljina railway line, which runs through the valley past Zitomislic, conveyed what were described as "six carloads of mothers, young girls and children. . .to Surmanci. . .they were led up the mountains and the mothers together with their children were thrown alive off the precipices" (Bishop Misic of Mostar, writing to the Archbishop Stepinac on 7 November 1941). The same bishop, in a letter to all his priests on 30 June that year, had asked them to say from their pulpits that those who murdered or misappropriated (i.e. stole) the possessions of others would not be granted absolution.

A rough translation of the words engraved on the column by the ravine – there is no cross here – reads:

> Glory to the victims of the Ustase, collaborators of the occupying enemy, who were in summer 1941 tortured most cruelly, killed, and thrown in this hole.

One Friday morning in November 1989 the sky was clear over Medjugorje. At Surmanci the sun shone and the air was still; yet the atmosphere seemed oppressive to the five people who had visited the convent of Zitomislic, and who now stood or knelt in silence as they contemplated that sudden and sharp-edged rocky ravine in which was a crater, its cover of concrete partially hidden by nature. The inscription was translated into English slowly and with hesitation by one of the two Croats present, while the others listened attentively – one Roman Catholic, two Anglicans –

before taking the path back to the road, still in silence. Next day, when they felt able to speak of it, they found that the experience had left them with a sense of great spiritual anguish but also, paradoxically, of utter peace and stillness. As one woman put it, ''they've gone on''. There were no ghosts.

There is an understandable reluctance on the part of those who live, work or minister in the locality to speak of Surmanci – and no doubt of many other places like it – or even to admit its existence. There seems also an unspoken wish to forget it, which may possibly conceal a disinclination to forgive. Mary Craig[1] quotes from the sermon of a bishop in Croatia at Christmas 1963, who spoke humbly of crimes committed by those who called themselves Catholic against Serbian Orthodox Christians, saying, ''We acknowledge with anguish the terrible crimes of these misguided men, and we beg our Orthodox brothers to forgive us, as Christ on the Cross forgave all men. We in our turn forgive all those who have wronged or hated us.'' These remarks caused outrage among the Croats, and some priests refused to read the letter from their own pulpits. But by October 1990 thoughts of forgiveness seemed equally far from the hearts of those Serbs who seized arms from police stations in Dalmatia, and were talking of a return of the Ustase regime.

April to June 1941 marked the beginning of the collaboration with the occupying Nazis of the Ustase rule. The perpetration of atrocities became almost

1 *Spark from Heaven*, Mary Craig. Hodder & Stoughton 1988.

commonplace; so that the incidents at Glina, Zitomislic and Surmanci, unbelievably shocking and terrible though they were, may be regarded as fairly typical of the time and place.

Yet they may have a particular significance.

Their occurrence forty years before the first Medjugorje vision could well be entirely fortuitous. What seems far less likely to be coincidental is the fact that the hills of Podbrdo and Surmanci are on one and the same mountain of Crnica and that the Virgin's first reported appearance on Podbrdo took place forty years to the day – *24 June* – after such crimes against humanity as those committed at Surmanci were made legal by Mile Budak's edict (page 122) becoming effective. Furthermore, at about the same time Father Jozo was made aware of the significance of forty years of Marshal Tito's Communist control (page 28).

Assuming the Six to be telling the truth, a consideration of the possibility of the monument at Surmanci accounting for the choice of Podbrdo as the site of the visions tends to give certain other things a rather sharper focus and clearer understanding; in particular, perhaps, the weeping Virgin's words to Marija on 26 June 1981, the third day of the visions: 'Peace. . .Be reconciled . . .' (page 25). A black cross marks the site of this encounter.

Then there is Krizevac (page2 41–42). That immense concrete cross built on Hercegovina's highest mountain-top, and so near that other mountain of Crnica, has been reverenced since 1933. Krizevac has been crowded every year from that date on Holy Cross day, which is observed by both Eastern and Western

Churches (and is included in the Anglican prayer book's calendar) every September; the day is kept in Medjugorje on the Sunday after 8 September, the crowds becoming immensely greater after the visions began in 1981. Yet the reverence inspired by this cross was very much part of life long before then in Medjugorje, whose people inscribed it in 1933 to the Redeemer of the human race as a sign of their faith, love and hope.

Do the events of Glina, Zitomislic and Surmanci symbolize some tremendous truth to which the far greater event of Podbrdo is pointing? Do these few square miles of sparsely inhabited plain and mountain, between the Christian East and West, represent or illustrate the time and place chosen by God to demonstrate the consequences for mankind of its wrong choices, and the possibilities for its right ones? And could these choices really be as simple as love or hate; peace or war; laughter or tears; joy or misery; forgiveness or punishment? And finally, is Medjugorje just a hoax on a rather grand scale, or will it continue to be a place of pilgrimage and a witness for all time to the truth of the Gospel of Christ?

PEOPLE AND PLACES

13
Two Friars and an Agnostic

This is about three men who have chosen to associate themselves with Medjugorje. Two are Franciscan priests, both of whom were born and bred near there; the other an English layman.

Father Slavko Barberic is persuaded of the authenticity of the visions: Father Ivo Sivric was determined to prove them fraudulent: Michael Jackson is an agnostic, who spent a week in Medjugorje in October 1989.

Father Slavko's investigations, begun in January 1982 (page 13), have led him on many journeys to many countries to speak in any of six languages, with reliable knowledge, of the events of Medjugorje. He still believes (July 1991) the Virgin Mary to be appearing there daily with messages from God to mankind, and he is saying in effect what Luther, founder of the Reformed Churches, understood and wrote in 1521: ''Mary does not desire to be an idol; she does nothing, God does all. We ought to call upon her, that for her

sake God may grant and do what we request.'' He
goes on to quote from St Paul to the Ephesians, ''He
is able to do above all that we ask – that is, he always
does more than we ask.''

Slavko points out that nature is available to all, and
that Mary appeared first on the hill, not in the church;
but that as a Mother, she will come where her children
are and was therefore still with them when in turn the
hill, the church and the rectory were forbidden to them
either by the Communists or the bishop. Her essential
message is of peace for all, not peace for the Catholic
Church alone. He remembers, too, that Milka and Ivan
were sorry to have seen the beautiful Lady once only,
and that Mirjana and Ivanka were sad when their
visions ended. All four could well have maintained that
they still saw her; but the fact that they did not do so
inclines him to the belief that, like the others, they
speak the truth. He also points out that the local history
was unknown to these children, who were too young
to have read of it.

From 18 August Father Tomislav Vlasic (page 36) was
with the Six daily, though initially not very impressed.
(''I already believe, my faith does not need these
apparitions.'') But when the children asked him to look
after them spiritually, he came to understand the
importance of the presence of the Virgin Mary in terms
of a much deeper faith, not only for himself. In
September 1985 he was transferred to the nearby
parish of Vitina, and from that time Slavko became and
has remained the children's spiritual adviser.

Probably because Tomislav has a particular rapport
with the pilgrims from Italy, an Association of the

Friends of Medjugorje in Milan published three volumes of Meditations, on talks given to various groups of people by Tomislav and Slavko. Known as the Grey, Blue and Red Books and dealing with Mary's messages from respectively Easter to December 1984, January to June, and July to December 1985, these books are distributed without charge in Italy; and to the British Isles, Canada, the U.S.A., Singapore and Australia in English translation. They are concerned less with the ongoing story of the visions, than with their deeper spiritual implications – to help and teach those who need a better understanding of the Virgin Mary's repeated request of ''Be converted'': not to the Catholic faith, but that all shall have faith in God. The editors of these talks, which have been transcribed from recordings, explain that ''there may be some imprecisions in the texts due to the fact that the Fathers have some difficulty in expressing themselves in Italian and that they were unable to correct the proofs''.

Because they are or have been in constant touch with the Six, these two friars must be in a better position than any others to interpret what the Six say Mary tells them, including the publicized messages. In 1988 Slavko wrote a pocket-sized prayer book and of this, with the other three, more will be said in chapters 15 to 18 dealing with the messages.

Regarding their characters, it is only necessary to meet the eyes and study the countenances of these two friars to be convinced that, whatever views they may hold, they cannot be liars. Of Father Slavko, it seems clear that he sustains with composure an average working day of eighteen or more hours; and that he combines intelligence of a high order with candour and a total lack of guile.

His response to the sound of whirring and clicking cameras in the church was to say with mild reproach, and first in English then in French, ''I called you here to pray, not to take photographs.'' He is at ease with the continual throng of cosmopolitan pilgrims and a still centre from which, with six other friars, the orderly crowds circulate, prayer is offered with reverence, and the church kept clean. Slavko's equilibrium, and his ability to combine availability with being in constant touch with the Six, is achieved only by strict personal prayer and fasting, thinks Laurentin; who comments that Medjugorje runs as smoothly as the shrine of Lourdes, where a hundred paid or voluntary helpers are employed.

Commenting on Mary's call to holiness, Slavko holds its meaning to be that we should live every day in the love of God and our fellows, and to pray that we can recognize God's will; so that the impossibly remote and daunting state of holiness becomes suddenly attainable.

The long duration of Mary's visits to Medjugorje he explains by an allegory of children asleep in a house on fire, whose mother ran to them, staying until they were saved. In the same way, God sends his own Mother to tell us, her children, that our house the world is on fire, and to save us from its destruction by, for instance, nuclear war or allowing our greed to ruin the good earth's resources.

Some of the ten secrets given to the Six and believed

to be apocalyptic warnings of the world's future, Slavko regards as road signs to avoid a crash – perhaps, for example, no entry, stop, single lane, keep right – intended to inspire care and hope of arrival rather than dread of annihilation – timely invitation for conversion to belief, not an announcement of catastrophe. By 1989 he looked on the eight visionary years in Medjugorje as labour pains before a birth already awaited for 3000 days, during which at least three hours of prayer were offered every evening in the church for a safe delivery. He believes in the power of prayer and that perhaps one day we shall be able to draw conclusions.

His close relationship with the visionaries is illustrated by his support of Ivanka's refusal to allow anyone but members of her own family to be present in 1990 during Mary's annual visit to her, conscious of the distress she experienced the previous year from cameras and crowds; and it was the Virgin's motherly intervention after Ivan's fall from grace (page 83) which warned him of the approach of an avenging angel in the shape of Slavko.

The likelihood of the vision being a counterfeit or mediumistic figure is, he thinks, an interesting hypothesis but one that fails to become a thesis since it cannot be proved. The possible presence of a ghost or medium personifying the mother-figure who weeps for human suffering, is discontinued by the behaviour of the Six, each of whom is absorbed in their own disparate life, unaware of and disinterested in either past or present history, and united as a group only by the vision. None but Vicka have experienced much in

the way of suffering. Medjugorje, though indeed
symbolic of extremes of human hope and suffering,
is not alone in this. Why, for instance, does no ghost
appear at places like Dachau?

He told a London audience in March 1990 that Mary
had not said convert to the Roman Catholic Church,
but surrender to God in prayer – advice whose origin
he did not doubt; and he regarded as corroboration
of her appearances the fact that he himself had never
seen her. This he thought a test of faith, since she had
not lacked opportunities on the thousands of occasions
at which he had been present when the Six claimed
to see her. If he, too, claimed to see her, he would at
once be suspected of subjectivity, if not collusion in
a dangerous deception. He remains objective, and sees
the vital importance of organizers and genuine
reporters being exact in the information they give, and
in avoiding the sensational.

Slavko takes a realistic view of Medjugorje's
transformation from a quiet hamlet, in whose few
homes the earlier pilgrims were made welcome in
exchange for little or no money. The same spirit of
service and hospitality motivates the great majority
in the present large and thriving community of
innkeepers who are necessary to sustain the
continuously oncoming daily thousands of pilgrims.
In terms of what may be happening, he sees a clear
analogy with the story of Martha (the housewife),
who was distracted with serving and of Mary (the
pilgrim), who chose to sit at Christ's feet and listen
to him; a better part only made possible by Martha's
"worry and fret about so many things". But St John

tells us that these two sisters were equally dear to Christ.[1]

By early 1987 government investment loans initiated new building, making pilgrim accommodation available within reach of the church and the two hills, but with two inevitable consequences for the local people: the necessity to prepare and serve food for their guests made church attendance difficult for them; and opportunists who were not necessarily devout seized the chance of reaping a good investment income by moving in on the Medjugorje scene, though it has to be said that the government takes sixty per cent of their profit in tax.

He considers another aspect to be reckoned with are the tourist agencies, who allot accommodation on commission and employ guide-interpreters who may be remote from any thought of Christianity. On the other hand, the role of Christian interpreter at Medjugorje is increasingly attracting young Yugoslav modern language graduates.

Slavko's investigations also led him to the discovery that many Medjugorje pilgrims came from curiosity, to have a look at a visionary, for the chance of a miracle or because a friend may have suggested it; but when asked why they came for a *second* time, 92 per cent said that it was to deepen their spiritual life. So it is the pilgrims who cause the explosion of buildings; a burst of sunshine which may create shadows but which may also, in time, provide the shade of the Oasis of Peace promised by Mary in a message of 26 June 1986.

1 Luke 10:38–42 and John 11:5.

Slavko is aware of the implications of Surmanci, as of the friars who joined the Ustase and of those at Siroki Brijeg whose pupils became Ustase leaders (pages 125–126). All are felt as a heavy burden which the Franciscans must carry; but which perhaps they can share with some of their Orthodox brother priests.

Fathers Slavko Barberic and Ivo Sivric both approached the Medjugorje phenomenon with a certain scepticism, though from rather different standpoints: Father Slavko with hope, that his doubts might be dispelled by objective analysis; Father Ivo with what appears to have been a subjective determination to prove his doubts well-founded.

This determination inspired him to give much time and trouble to the publication of Volume I of his *The Hidden Side of Medjugorje* (page 62), a careful study of which fails, however, to justify his contention that the Six are imposters.

The author of the prospective Volume II of this work is Louis Bélanger, editor of Volume I, whose identification of the supposed vision of Mary as a mischievous and menacing entity clearly carries weight with Father Ivo. Bélanger accuses Father Slavko of the bias of belief in God; Laurentin takes note of Bélanger's conviction that God, Christ and the Blessed Virgin are myths, quoting him as arguing that ''Only a study which gave a natural explanation, foreign to faith, would be objective. Scientific thesis forbids God to make miracles. . .and Christ and the Blessed Virgin from manifesting themselves.'' This view implies a curious contradiction, since by attributing to science the ability to control the heavenly hierarchy, he acknowledges that they cannot be myths.

Objectivity or lack of bias therefore seems to present problems to both Father Ivo and his editor, though again from different standpoints; Bélanger is an avowed atheist, Sivric an ordained Christian priest. A strange alliance. Laurentin's reference to Bélanger's skilful recruitment of Sivric to further his own parapsychological studies may to some extent explain this alliance, particularly in the context of Sivric's careful selection of source material to support a negative view of the Medjugorje events: a view which, combined with financial difficulties, is thought to account for the delayed publication of Volume II.

Comparatively little is known of Father Ivo Sivric's personality. Some members of his family in Medjugorje, who know him well and at one time saw him frequently, found that his visits to them had ceased by 1990. This they put down to local adverse reactions to his negative attitude to the Six and their story, and to the fact that he relied in his researches on second-hand information. He also, of course, found ready cooperation in his attitude from the bishop (chapter 4), who welcomed him as an ally.

His positive contributions include, in sixteen appendices to his book, interviews from 27 to 30 June 1981. These conversations with the friars then in Medjugorje – Fathers Zrinko Cuvalo and Jozo Zovko – record their attempts to establish, with the six children, what was in fact taking place on Podbrdo during the first week. The originals of these cassettes were removed by the police when Jozo was arrested in August (page 66). The copies, quoted by Father Ivo, have always been available to and used by researchers, though not hitherto published in English. Father Ivo also took a cool look at the possibility that the vision or apparition may represent Satan disguised as an angel of light in terms of 2 Corinthians 11:14-15; and in Laurentin's view his intentions may have been peaceful, though obscured by Bélanger's controversial translation and editing from Croat to French, and from French to English. As to this, Bélanger states that Father Ivo's manuscript reached him with the comment: ''If I had written favourably and without critical examination, I would have no difficulty in finding a publisher. What, then, do you suggest?'' What he suggested was a collaboration which would ''perfect our respective theological and psychological points of view. . .to plumb the depths of Medjugorje's events''.

Volume II is awaited.

Father Ivo's decision to undertake a critical examination of these events commands respect, and must have great importance from the hand of a Croat Fransciscan. Indeed, such an examination may be long overdue, given that what has so far been published tends towards an enthusiasm not always tempered by caution. Against that, his findings can only be considered in the light of his acceptance of second-hand information; the possibly understandable loyalty to his Communist relatives which appears to inform his negative bias (pages 65–66); his fairly consistently defamatory comments on other priests engaged in seemingly honourable and devout research (Fathers

Vlasic, Zovko and Laurentin); and his condemnation as propaganda of ''all of the books and articles written by proponents of Medjugorje. . .the majority of these works are slanted and superficial''.

Because Father Ivo is troubled about many things concerning Medjugorje, he is personally unable to believe that the Virgin is present in these manifestations. They have not as yet shown themselves to be evil.

In his Appendix 17, Father Ivo makes some very relevant and interesting observations about private revelations and apparitions, quoting from such respected contemporary Catholic theologians as Karl Rahner S.J. and Edward Schillebeeckx, and agreeing with Rahner that there is more danger of error in credulity than in scepticism.

He notes that Thomas Aquinas (died 1274) maintained that ''Christ, after his Ascension, rarely appeared in his person; he merely appeared in a visible form, but not in his real body'', and that in this context the modern A. Tanquerey wrote: ''What had been said of Our Lord applies also to the Blessed Virgin.'' Further, if public revelation ended with the last apostle, Rahner holds that private revelations are 'the impulse of the Holy Spirit. It is well known that reference to God's commanding something in a vision is more efficacious than the best exposition of general principles.'' Father Ivo concedes that this cannot be totally denied, while warning of bogus visions; and that those involved in apparitions have too often been driven by emotion, wishful thinking, pious initiative, personal turmoil or worse.

Schillebeeckx identifies authentic visions and private revelations as small signs and tokens of God's love; and that they should be neither exaggerated nor underestimated, since they point to God's love for us only in order to draw our attention to Jesus Christ. In Schillebeeckx's view, authentic apparitions are to be accepted with faith "on the authority of the visionaries themselves, whose worthiness of belief has been subjected to critical investigation".

Father Ivo also notes, however, that theologians are not always in agreement (he is himself a theologian), and that Rahner's definition of prophetism includes not only those who have private visions but also those who play the devil's advocate or negator; and that the unmasking of false prophecy can itself be a prophetic mission.

Perhaps the role of devil's advocate (page 61) should not be taken too lightly.

Born in 1962, Michael Jackson is a life-long agnostic; but his boyhood interest in the experience of nature mystics influenced his later decision to read psychology and philosophy as an Oxford undergraduate. In 1991 he finished writing a doctoral thesis on the paradoxical relationship between psychotic and healthy transcendent perception, or the nature of mental illness in the context of religious experience. This has intensified his interest in spirituality and his awareness of its underlying mystery, an effect which contributed to his decision to go to Medjugorje in 1989.

Ambivalence is probably the word which best describes his reactions to the week he spent there. He may have encountered the *mystery* of a faith which can "prove the existence of the realities that at present remain unseen[2]", but for him that faith remains a mystery. He accepts that God is incomprehensible from a human point of view; that though others may have experienced the reality of God, such an insight has so far been denied to him; and that if he decides to seek God, his search is unlikely to end in any institutional Church.

From his researches, Mike defines psychosis as a state of being out of touch with the consensual view of reality, with a consequent difficulty in living a normal life. The positive symptoms are delusions or hallucinations, most commonly diagnosed as schizophrenia; but he notes that someone reporting a spiritual or religious experience does not lose touch with reality; and that though brief the experience is usually unique, transforming and life-enhancing in a way which may enable the person to come to terms with difficulties in their personal life.

He considers that circumstances dictate whether people have psychotic rather than spiritual experiences and that, for example, a visionary whose reported experiences were discounted might become psychotic. This theory is not proved, however, by the Medjugorje Six, who were from the outset indifferent to public opinion because in no doubt of the veracity of their experience. Mike makes the further interesting point that had there been one visionary, rather than six who supported each other, their reaction might have been less composed; yet the behaviour of the single

2 Hebrews 11:1.

visionary of Lourdes (chapter 14) remained consistently
calm and normal, despite the medical and police
harassment to which she and the Six were all
subjected.

Among other interesting theories, he contends that
it is possible to translate the distinguishing marks of
a spiritual experience into psychiatric symptoms,
making a comparison between the revelation given
through a spiritual experience with the delusions
suffered in schizophrenia. Diagnosis may become a
question of interpretation therefore, and a psychiatrist
who may also be an agnostic or atheist may lack the
data by which to identify an encounter with God. But
of a thousand confidential written accounts of religious
experience which were received by the Alister Hardy
Research Centre, he found that only 15 per cent
"showed at least one fairly unambiguously psychiatric
symptom". In writing of the great personal significance
of these confidential accounts, many of the authors said
that a fear of ridicule or of being thought mentally
unsound had prevented them speaking of the
experience to *anyone*, although half the adult
population of this country are believed to have had
such an experience; which may imply a risk of faulty
diagnosis which they are not prepared to take.

Mike found that before attempting to assess the
message of Medjugorje it was necessary to learn
something of the Christian message, particularly what
he saw as the profundities and contradictions of the
Roman Catholic version of it.

He was also faced with what struck him as the visible
contradiction of the sacred and profane: for example,

his recognition of Podbrdo and Krizevac as holy places, yet their desecration by the litter of empty bottles and waste paper; the sanctity of the church, yet approached past unremoved debris. Here perhaps was the ambivalence of intelligent observation and deduction, which was nevertheless blind to the possible co-existence and interaction of faith in everyday life; or the likely effects of the cause of a divine revelation, though this could at best be regarded as fantasy, or as ideal rather than real. Yet Everest is among many desecrated mountain-tops; and no doubt the approach road to the church will be smartened up when the still available building space has been made use of; the population of a village or two has come to terms with being overtaken by an annual ten million or more pilgrims; the threatened town planning is a fact of life; and what an architect describes as the ecological time-bomb of Medjugorje has been defused.

Mike was deterred on arrival in Medjugorje by the commercialism of ''a row of brand new bars and shops, with flashing neon signs, and glitzy exteriors, lined with rosaries and plastic Madonnas with removable heads''; and he was not surprised that the (Communist) government had ceased to oppose the apparitions for commercial rather than *spiritual* reasons. He disliked the eruption of tourism, the pilgrim accommodation which scarred the landscape, and the sophisticated modern coaches cluttering rural lanes. Yet commercialism is always an inescapable concomitant of pilgrim needs and demands, including the necessity of feeding and housing them; and the explosion of commercialism could as easily be interpreted as an acknowledgement of the mystical message and a sign of hope.

Mike's acerbic reactions may be a good and necessary antidote to the cloying credulity too often to be found; though there is a lingering suspicion that for him the essential wood, though present, is obscured by the trees – a suspicion borne out, perhaps, by a determination to discuss Medjugorje and not Christianity. Probably what he most disliked was the dogmatism he found among some of the people he encountered. An emphasis on obedience, not simply to God but to the Church, the Pope and the priests, repelled him – an attitude on the part of both certain clergy and laity which he thought conflicted, in its failure to transcend religious divisions, with the main Medjugorje message of peace.

He was impressed by the strength of conviction of an Irishman who spoke of his instant conversion to belief and his sudden understanding of the power of prayer; and by Vicka's enthusiasm, warmth and complete confidence in her God, though what she told the pilgrims he found uncompelling. But he perfectly understood a fellow-pilgrim who afterwards wrote: "Medjugorje. . .is a place full of love, peace, beauty, calmness and most importantly God"; and he was aware of people, both living in and visiting Medjugorje, who "seemed to have achieved an enviable degree of inner calm, reconciliation and profound faith, at least partly through their experience at Medjugorje".

The Irishman said that his strong faith was now like that of a sheep. Reflecting on this statement Mike questions why, if God wanted us to be sheep, did he make us into people? And is it necessarily better to be a contented sheep rather than an unhappy philosopher? But it seems possible that an unhappy philosopher might not have understood what St John was talking about in his allegory of The Good Shepherd[3] who leads his sheep to safe pasture. The sheep follow him because they know his voice . . .

3 John 10:1–16.

14
Lourdes, Fatima and Kibeho

Stories of visions of the Mother of God or the Blessed Virgin Mary, though familiar and often encouraging to many of those who belong to the Eastern Orthodox or Roman Catholic Churches, may sound strange, daunting or even rather alarming to others, who therefore dismiss suggestions or visiting places where these visions are said to have occurred.

Supernatural manifestations of one kind or another, however, tend to have a universal appeal; so that reports of ghosts or apparitions may draw the curious to those localities, with the idea of ridiculing or possibly experiencing the wonder for themselves. The decisive factor is probably only found at the place in question, where a ghostly presence, visible or not, may induce a sensation of cold and a *frisson* of dread; while conversely warmth, confidence and an awesome certainty of truth is often experienced at the place of vision, where many who go to mock may stay to venerate.

There is nothing new in the reporting of visions of Mary; indeed, it was estimated in 1986 that she has appeared 21,000 times in the past ten centuries. Most of these reports have certain things in common, in particular the initial unease they cause the Roman Catholic Church, and the extreme caution with which that Church proceeds before pronouncing that such visions may be accepted as authentic. Such approval has been given in the case of Lourdes and Fatima, though not so far for Kibeho, (Key *bay* oh).

Lourdes and Fatima are probably the best known Marian sanctuaries in the world and now equalled by Medjugorje where, as Slavko pointed out in September 1990, pilgrims no longer seem interested in whether or not a bishop's Commission is prepared to authenticate the events. The miracles of conversion there startle the many priests of all nations who hear confessions and can no longer doubt the presence of God in that place.

Lourdes seems to be regarded as a point of reference; for example Medjugorje is described as the modern Lourdes, and Kibeho may become the ''Lourdes of Africa'', implying that what appeared to be supernatural healing was received at those two places also. At each place the vision was seen only by adolescents or small children. The obvious innocence of these chosen children was untainted by worldly experience or influence, and combined in each case with a simple, unpretentious and essentially normal background. This rendered them capable of relating to or being identified with the great majority of people of all nationalities in any age, who could accept without too much question the simplicity, purity and truth of what the children said they had seen and heard. If they were indeed chosen, who better than these children to reveal the mystery of the kingdom of heaven, the Good News revealed to the simple, for which Christ blessed the "Lord of heaven and earth, for hiding these things from the learned and clever and revealing them to mere children" as page 72 (St Matthew 11:25, Luke 10:21, Mark 10:14–15).

The well-known story of Lourdes in France is based on the words and actions of one totally illiterate, though not unintelligent, girl named Bernadette Soubirous. She was fourteen years old one cold February morning of 1858 when she heard a strong wind; she saw that it blew on a wild rose bush in a cave by the river, but failed to stir the leaves of nearby poplar trees. Suddenly she saw the dark cave fill with golden light, and on the rose bush stood a "white girl".

There seemed no reason or motive for Bernadette to have invented this scene, even if she had been capable of doing so, wildly improbable as it was. She was both scared and thrilled, though unaware of the symbolism which may have occurred to some of those who heard the story: the powerful wind of Pentecost which preceded the light of the Holy Spirit, and filled the house where the twelve apostles had met; perhaps the same wind and light that filled a cave to draw attention to a rose bush, source of the Virgin Mary's ancient emblem of the mystic rose of purity and paradise; and finally the rosary prayer circlet which the white girl showed Bernadette only after she had taken her own rosary beads from her pocket. She saw the vision of the white girl eighteen times, referring to it in her native patois as "Aquerò", meaning it or that thing; and never, during many interrogations, did she claim to have seen the Virgin Mary.

The figure in white spoke to Bernadette, always coming to her surrounded by golden light, though invisible and inaudible to any but herself; and though Bernadette was always willing to answer questions, she was not concerned to persuade anyone of what she saw, though constantly asking the white girl to say who she was. This question was not answered until 25 March or Lady Day, the date on which the Angel Gabriel's announcement to Mary is remembered. After an interval of three weeks without visions, Bernadette felt a strong compulsion to go early to the cave that day, when for the first time Aquerò was there before her; and this time the question was answered. The words given her, which Bernadette was to say she had never heard before, were spoken in the familiar patios with which the vision always addressed her, rather than in the formal French she might have heard in church; and they represented the dogma defined by the Roman Catholic Church in 1854, after many centuries of theological argument and a little less than four years before Aquerò's appearance: '*I am the Immaculate Conception.*' Probably no other words would have so instantly convinced the sceptical Dean Peyramale, who had repeatedly told Bernadette to ask the lady her name, and to whom Bernadette reported the words she had memorized between the cave and the priest's house.

The only signs and portents at Lourdes for anyone

but Bernadette were the sight of her in ecstasy on 7 April, when she felt no pain from the flame of a large candle which failed to burn her cupped hands during the penultimate vision; and her discovery, with guidance from the vision, of the spring of water which still rises continuously from the floor of the cave, supplying the healing water which the pilgrims may drink, bathe in and take home in bottles.

The crowds who attended Bernadette on her visits to the cave could only guess from her rapt expression when the ''white girl'' was with her, just as the transfigured faces of the Six in Medjugorje and the Seven in Kibeho signalled Mary's arrival to the onlookers there. Bernadette's ecstasies lasted for as much as an hour, during which time she was unaware of surrounding noise or people, and became too heavy for a strong man to lift, small for her age though she was.

It may be remembered that when Father Jozo learned that the Medjugorje children knew nothing of Marian visions he lent them a book about Lourdes (page 68), and it was this that convinced them that the visions would cease after the eighteenth appearance.

Bernadette learned to read and write, and became a nun. She died on 16 April 1879, having made her final vows the previous September; and in 1933 she was canonized. Medical examination found her to be physically and mentally sound; and those who are uninfluenced by Catholic dogmas may possibly agree with the bishop who said, ''A simple, uncultured peasant-girl such as this could not possibly have imagined it all.''

Fatima in Portugal is known and honoured, at least by Roman Catholics, for the behaviour and reports in 1917 of three small and quite illiterate children; and for the startling and unexpected signs and portents which were taken as substantiation of their story, and have become known as "The Miracle of The Sun". The children were Lucia aged ten, Francisco, eight and his sister Jacinta, seven. Lucia was alive in 1991, a nun then aged eighty-three; Francisco died in 1919 and his sister Jacinta in 1920.

Whereas Mary may have appeared eighteen times to Bernadette, these three children say that she came to them only six times from May to October; but like the Medjugorje Six, they knew nothing of Lourdes. As was the case with Bernadette, their parents were humble, lived frugally from force of circumstances, never missed Sunday Mass and always prayed together as a family; and like Bernadette they carried rosary beads in their pockets. All this was, however, the culture and tradition of both places at the times in question.

The Fatima children spent their days as shepherds, accustomed to saying grace after their bread and cheese lunch on the hillsides. They were occupied with the sheep at noon when the vision came to them for the first time, and as at Lourdes it was heralded by an apparent change in the weather: not by a strong wind blowing only in a cave, but by lightning from a clear sky. They ran to some trees for cover, before the expected thunderstorm; but at another flash of light their eyes were drawn to a holm-oak sapling about four feet high, above which stood a smiling and beautiful woman. She radiated bright light, wore a white dress and said gently, "Do not be afraid", the words Mary heard when the Angel Gabriel was sent to her by God.

In Lourdes the vision was silent until her third appearance, when Bernadette was persuaded by others to ask for her name in writing. The response was "It is not necessary" followed by "Will you be kind enough to come here for a fortnight?" When at noon on Sunday 13 May 1917 Lucia asked the lady on the sapling where she came from the answer was "Heaven", followed by a request to the children to return there at noon on the thirteenth day of the next five months, when the lady would say who she was.

None of these children were afraid, nor did they feel any restraint on their freedom of choice. After a brief initial panic they were eager to see and hear the lovely lady again, serenely happy in her presence, and much surprised by the great courtesy and consideration with which she treated them. This was equally true of the Medjugorje children.

When Bernadette and the Medjugorje Six (apart from the first week) spoke to the vision no one else could hear what they said, although they themselves thought they were speaking normally and audibly; but at Fatima the crowd round the children could hear the one-sided conversation of Lucia's words only. Francisco could only see the lady, Jacinta saw and heard her, but was too shy to speak.

The three children returned to the holm-oak bush at noon on the thirteenth of June, July, September and October, each time warned by a flash of light in the sky before the arrival of what they described as "a lady all of light", so bright that it hurt their eyes. All that was seen by the increasingly large crowds was a small cloud floating down from the east, to settle on the tree before disappearing again upwards and eastward to cries from Lucia of "There she goes!", (compare with "*Ode!*" page 23) when there was a sound like a distant rocket. On 13 September thousands saw a globe of light in place of the cloud: but there were greater signs to come.

The children were not by the tree on 13 August, having been abducted that morning by the mayor of Ourem, where they were interrogated and threatened: treatment also suffered by the visionaries of Lourdes and Medjugorje. At noon that day the waiting crowds all heard a loud clap of thunder, *followed* by lightning, not preceded as normally. When a small white cloud settled on the tree and then disappeared into the sky, the people and landscape were suddenly transformed. Rainbow colours were reflected from faces and clothes, each leaf on the trees seemed a bright flower and the ground was a mosaic of colour.

Perhaps because they were prevented from going to the holm-oak on 13 August, the vision came to the children at a different place six days later, when the lady promised them a miracle in October "so that everyone can believe in the apparitions": and so it was.

On 13 October the now familiar cloud was seen to settle on the bush, as Lucia was heard to say once more, "What do you want of me?" "A chapel in honour of the Lady of the Rosary", she was told, before the bright vision disappeared heavenwards for the last time. Then the children described seeing in the sky wonderful tableaux of the Holy Family, though like the Lady of the Rosary invisible to all others. Simultaneously the enthralled crowd watched for about ten minutes as the sun appeared to spin like a wheel of fire, covering the earth and themselves with shafts of coloured light like whirling rainbows; then falling towards the now terrified people before resuming its normal place in the sky. These sights were corroborated by various people who watched them at some distance from Fatima, which seems to eliminate mass hallucination as an explanation. Nothing abnormal was recorded by any observatory.

Historically, the visionary appearances in these three places all occurred during times of public denials of Christ. At Lourdes in 1858 the effects of the abolition of religion during the French Revolution were still being felt. In Portugal the republican regime of 1910 had boasted that the practice of religion would soon cease, the mayor who abducted the Fatima children having been a Marxist. In Yugoslavia, just over a year after the death of Marshal Tito, the Communist government were ready to construe as insurrection any overt demonstrations of religious belief. In all three places the children concerned endured police interrogation and intimidation.

At the second Fatima vision of June 1917 Lucia quoted Mary as saying, ''I want you to learn to read''; and when the visions had ceased Lucia did so, eventually writing her memoirs. The seven young people who spoke of their visionary experiences in Kibeho were all literate, four of them still at school when their visions began on 28 November 1981 only a few months after the first reported appearances at Medjugorje in June of that year.

Kibeho in Rwanda, Central Africa became Christian at the end of the nineteenth century. It is believed to be the first place in Africa to report visions of the Virgin; and in view of her message of 2 May 1982 in Medjugorje — ''I have come to call the world to conversion for the last time. I will not appear any more on this earth'' — it may also be the last. A rugged and mountainous country, its two rival tribes have been fighting for supremacy at least since 1959, leading to civil war in 1990. A year or so before the visions began there had been an outbreak of iconoclasm in Rwandan churches and at crossroads, when pictures and statues of the Virgin were stolen, damaged or destroyed, causing much distress to the faithful. Against this background, it was thought Mary had come to offer consolation and encouragement, in a poor school in what was the poorest part of the country.

Apart from the same urgent message for peace and prayer, there are few similarities with Medjugorje, where the Six were all under eighteen years old and only one, Vicka, was seventeen when the visions began. Four of the Africans were under seventeen, three being over twenty; and the vision appeared to each of them separately, never together as a group, and seldom daily. In Medjugorje after the first week Mary's daily visits were private in the sense that the onlookers could hear nothing; in Kibeho they were very public, lasting sometimes for over an hour, during which time the visionaries' audible words were amplified to the listening crowd of people.

Unlike Medjugorje, the bishop of this African diocese is impressed by the reverence and renewed faith of the many pilgrims, by medical and theological tests, and by the integrity of the visionaries and of the French priest who decided to write of them, French being the official language of the country. This priest does not live in Kibeho, but is fluent in the written and spoken Rwanda language, and was therefore able to relate to the visionaries and their culture. But he is not moved by the marvellous or extraordinary, nor dependent on miracles for faith; and with the mocking response of ''We can telephone Heaven!'', he regarded as naïve and gullible the fellow-priest who first told him what was happening. But having spent time at Kibeho in the course of ten more journeys, by 1984 he had changed his mind.

Alphonsine, a girl aged sixteen in November 1981, was the first and also the last to see the vision. A pupil in a girl's boarding school run by Rwandan nuns, she was helping in the refectory at the midday meal when she heard a voice call, ''My child''. Like the boy Samuel she answered, ''Here I am'' before kneeling, crossing herself and saying, ''Who are you?'' The surprising reply was, ''I am the Mother of the Word.'' St John 1:1 is relevant:

In the beginning was the Word
The Word was with God and the Word was God

words quoted in the Memorare (chapter 19). They happen also to represent the patron saint of the parish, though it is a title scarcely known in Rwanda or even to the majority in Kibeho.

Alphonsine said the vision disappeared heavenwards (as at Medjugorje and Fatima, though it is unlikely that she had then heard of either). Like Bernadette she was transfixed and immovable in ecstasy but she was thought to have been bewitched, particularly as she came from an area renowned for the African preoccupation with witchcraft.

Mary appeared to Alphonsine again the next day, but the nuns still disbelieved her story and her fellow pupils ridiculed and mocked this crank – for example with cries of ''Kneel down! You'll have a vision!'' There were two Protestants on the staff of this Roman Catholic college and seventeen others among the pupils; and when the January to April term began, *all* the pupils were determined to uncover this great deception. Though it was obvious Alphonsine was speaking to someone, no one else could hear the other side of the conversation and neither staff nor pupils were prepared to believe that the Mother of God spoke to Alphonsine unless she also appeared to others.

When, therefore, Mary became visible and audible to *five* other girls – two in the same college, three in a primary school – both schools and populace responded with uninhibited joy, expressed by Catholics and Protestants alike with typically African singing and dancing and an upsurge of renewed belief in the Gospel.

These five said they first saw Mary in January, March, May, July and August of 1982, but the visions had ceased for all but Alphonsine by December 1983. Alphonsine continued to see and hear Mary until January 1986, then on the anniversary date of 28

November until 1989, when to her great sorrow the visions ceased. She regarded Mary as a Mother, who looked like a local person (Alphonsine lived with her own mother, her parents having separated) and who spoke to her in her own language, as with the Six of Medjugorje; but she could not describe the colour of Mary's skin, except to say that she was not white as represented in pictures, nor black nor half-caste. She wore a seamless white dress and veil but no shoes; and she "glided like a bird. . .in the midst of flowers, incomparably lovely".

Mary appeared to Alphonsine on most Saturdays from December 1982 in a dormitory during the evening; but from difficulties caused by people converging on the school, from 16 January 1983 the visions took place out of doors in the school yard. In time Mary became the loving Mother of all the pupils, speaking to them through the visionaries and sharing not only their prayers but their problems, joys, and regrets.

The general public who had come long distances were able to follow what the six girls said. The visionaries stood, in turn, on a railed-off platform the better to be seen and heard; and it was not long before the people who were sceptical or merely curious became pilgrims, listening to the messages, praying and offering petitions and thanksgiving. The six visionaries never saw the Virgin simultaneously but each in turn, which had the effect of prolonging the event from early afternoon to late at night. Private visions continued in the dormitory, where a space had been cleared to act as a chapel: the date of the public visions was made known in advance, and the crowds who came stood listening and attentive for many hours.

These six girls had been brought up as Christians, but the boy Segatashya, a shepherd aged fifteen in July 1982, was born to pagan parents. The news that Christ had appeared to him spread like a bush fire, though it was not taken seriously, since before the vision the boy knew nothing of the Gospel, had never set foot in a church, and was illiterate. But when the onlookers heard him talking about forgiveness and charity, and saying the Lord's prayer and the Gospel prayers of the rosary, the representative gatherings to hear him grew larger and they listened in awe.

Initially Segatashya was startled by hearing a voice, and then by the materialization of a man with a black skin like his own but in a dazzling light, and dressed as a Rwandan with a loincloth. When he asked, "Who are you?" he was told, "I am called Jesus", after which this figure appeared often to Segatashya; and though he also saw Mary, it seems that it was Christ who gave him the knowledge necessary for his baptism at Pentecost in June 1983. By that Easter he had learned to read and write in three months, having never before been to school, and after baptism his name was changed to Emmanuel (meaning God with us) as Jesus had requested. His instruction for baptism and confirmation was completed in nine months, a course for which four years was normally allowed.

This boy is believed to have been given a missionary message by Christ, to be taken to neighbouring countries and throughout Rwanda when he came of age; and to this call he has chosen to respond.

Of the Kibeho visionaries the parish priest who had followed the events closely could only say, "They have seen a person who speaks in the name of the Gospel." Many witnesses of various occupations wrote of their own change of heart as a result of this, including the professor of French at the college; who said that just as a child is glad to think about his mother, so the thought of Mary brightened his existence: and in the context of the prodigal son "God does not abandon his child: he awaits his return". Emmanuel speaks of Christ's return and of the need to be prepared for it. These may be the first and last times that Mary will appear in Africa (page 65), but the visions may also be very significant for the simple acceptance by the people of that great continent of the truth of the Gospel, particularly as Emmanuel is among those who says he was apprised of Christ's return to earth.

Apart from people seen to be in mystical ecstasy, from signs in the sky and from medically inexplicable cures, factors common to all these places seem to be the great peace, joy and certainty experienced by all the visionaries concerned, and the spiritual repercussions of an explosion of faith, as at Medjugorje, which brings with it peace of soul and the mutual love and cooperation of believers, not only with each other but for what each person sees as the will of God for themselves.

All these visionaries have progressed in literacy. The times of the appearances have also moved forward – from morning at Lourdes, noon at Fatima, evening at

Medjugorje and nightfall at Kibeho – and so, it seems, has the scope of the messages, which at Lourdes and Fatima were addressed implicitly to the predominantly Roman Catholic believers of those parts of Catholic Europe.

But on 29 June 1981 the visionary lady told the Medjugorje Six ''There is only one God and one Faith''; and in July 1982-3 a Kibeho African girl heard her say, ''Before God there is neither Protestant nor Catholic, nor Adventist, nor Moslem, nor any branch of other creeds. . .the true son of God is whoever does God's will.'' Commenting on this, the Catholic priest who wrote of the Kibeho events said, ''The Virgin Mary never asked the Protestant or Moslem pupils to become Catholic but to recognize her as the Mother of God'', which has implications echoed by Slavko in 1990, when he told some London listeners (page 38) that Mary had not said that all must convert to the Roman Catholic Church.

THE MESSAGES

15
"My Angels"

This is the loving and maternal way in which the six chosen children say that the Virgin spoke to them from the second day, 25 June 1981 when she left them with ''Goodbye, my Angels'', a farewell to be repeated each day; and heard with much joy. The Six may indeed be God's angels or messengers, chosen perhaps for their unsullied youth and normality, their serenity and Christian upbringing, and their ignorance of power politics: clean slates on which to write a clear message of God's commands.

They were typical of immature visionaries throughout the world, whose basic characteristics have been found to include a rural background, modest means and education, and a lack of travel. When reminded later of that second day, Mirjana pointed out that they were from a small village and, unlike many young people from America or Europe, home, school and family was their life.

On day five, all that ten-year-old Jakov remembered hearing her say was ''You are my Angels, my dear Angels'', and as she vanished, ''Go in God's peace'', the blessing with which she was always to leave them. On the same evening Ivanka asked if she wished them to pray or sing, to be told "Both. Pray and sing, my dear Angels."

In questioning them during the first week, the priests referred to the vision as that ghost (or the *Gospa* or ghost), asking if they were not afraid that she might deceive them and not return the next day as promised. Ivanka's response was that "she never deceived us and she is not going to deceive us", showing the total trust, confidence and lack of fear with which the vision inspired them, a trust which had not been betrayed by 1991. Laurentin found that they regarded her as their special mother, the words "my Angels" having an intimate and tender Croat connotation that cannot be expressed in English – or presumably French.

Talking to Gitta Sereny of the *Sunday Times* in October 1985, Slavko said that it could not at that time be proved that the Six were seeing the Virgin, only that they were not lying; and that when they say they hear her speak in their own language, it may not mean that she speaks at all. They are enabled to see and hear her, together or separately, speaking about such mundane things as school, besides such philosophical, moral and political things as the future of the world. But he says it must not be forgotten "that these enormously complex subjects are being communicated to very simple young people with limited knowledge and imagination, and only basic vocabulary". How it can all happen only God knows, said Slavko with a smile.

They do not memorize or write word for word the

messages they hear, but recount them to the priest who advises them, normally Father Slavko, in their own words each according to their temperament and understanding, and with theological interpretation from a friar. The discernment of the thirteenth-century St Thomas Aquinas is probably still valid: ''Whatever is received is received according to the measure of the receiver.''

How accurate can these purported messages really be? None of the children could or can write shorthand; so that what was heard was transmitted both orally or in writing, at once or after a certain delay, directly or indirectly, dependent on the urgencies or distractions of the moment. To these hazards must be added the need for and achievement of almost immediate translation and transmission in many languages, with the inevitable discrepancies which occur in the many English versions, if in no others.

The Six have always maintained that they hear and speak to Mary as in normal conversation. The true message is perhaps contained clearly and simply in her faithful, almost daily presence for over ten years, her patient repetition of the word Peace and her admonition to Be Converted. If the Vision is indeed Mary, the purpose of all this can only be to remind us of Christ and to re-state the Gospel – indeed, this is the *effect* of the visions, whether of the Virgin Mary or not, and whether they are happening or not.

The meaning of the word Conversion in this context was clearly defined by Jakov, then aged about nineteen. It means, he said, to *experience* God, rather than going dutifully to church: it is God living within

him, and he being aware of this. It is given as a result
of prayer, which is dialogue with God, and in Holy
Communion when Christ is received as bread and
wine by each communicant. This, he believes, explains
the Virgin's appearances: she is here to teach this
awareness of the presence of God within each person
on earth, though each is given the choice of receiving
or rejecting God.

Vicka's interpretation is that all are born with a
knowledge of God, that each has his own way to pray,
and that Mary's messages are for everyone. This truth
was conveyed to the Rev. Stanley Jones, a Methodist
missionary, while proclaiming Christ to a mixed group
of people in India. A venerable Hindu said, "Sir, I
thank you. I have known him all my life and now you
have told me his name,"[1] which may have some
relevance to Mary's message of 29 June 1981 (page 30),
"There is only one God, one faith."

The greeting in Medjugorje, honoured by long usage
and still current, is "Praised be Jesus and Mary" with
the response of "Forever". Mary's greeting to the Six
is said always to have been "Praised be Jesus" and
her farewell "Go in God's peace."

'Dear Children' is claimed as the prefix to all Mary's
messages to the Six, who say that they experience joy
in her presence, long for her return each day and are
desolate at the prospect of the end of her visits. But
there are obstacles on this path to peace and joy, and
Mary warns her Angels of the tireless activity and
relentless influence of Satan, that force of evil

1 A story told by Robert Llewelyn.

constantly warring against the power of good or God, and against the fulfilment of the Virgin's entreaty to Marija on day three of, "Peace. Be reconciled with God and each other" (page 25).

" . . .Satan disguises himself as an angel of light",[2] which prompted Father Jozo to ask Mirjana and Ivanka on day five if they were not afraid that Satan could pretend, and say, "I am the Blessed Virgin Mary", but they told him they knew, probably rightly, that the devil would run away from prayer and holy water (pages 24 and 25). Mirjana was yet to encounter the devil, as described on page 76.

She gave the Six much advice in the matter, as for example on 29 October and 6 December 1981, 11 February 1982, 4 September 1986 and 25 September 1987:

You, my Angels, be on your guard. There is enough mendacious news . . .

Be strong and persevering. My dear Angels, go in the peace of God.

Pray my Angels, persevere! Do not let the enemy take possession of you in anything. Be courageous.

Dear Children, Satan lies in wait for each of you. He tries, each day, to plant doubts in each of you.

Dear Children, Satan is strong, and he watches over each of you in order to tempt you. Pray, and this way he will not be able to harm you nor block your way . . .

2 Corinthians 11:14.

16
Thursdays

Writing of the Greek Orthodox visionary Vassula Ryden (born 18 June 1942), married with two children, who in September 1985 began to write words she believed to be given to her in dialogue with Christ, Laurentin wrote: "Experience has taught me that visionaries, even true ones, are not infallible. We must be careful. A lot of Christians are not attracted by private revelations. They find that the Gospel is sufficient." He goes on to point out that even if all the marks of a genuine visionary or spiritual communication seem to be present, no one is compelled to accept them as true; but that Vassula's mission about which she is diffident, is to proclaim *unity*. This may be a part of the progression from Pentecostalism, the Charismatic Renewal, and the "New Pentecost" for which Pope John XXIII prayed at the Second Vatican Council, whose goal was the unity of all Christians (pages 34–35).

In the matter of fallible visionaries, perhaps their interrogators should not be discounted. For example, in *Queen of the Cosmos*, Jan Connell (see bibliography)

– who is described as a lawyer pursuing a logical line of questioning – asked the visionary Marija "Is the message for Hindus and Buddhists, for Jews and Protestants, Moslems and Atheists?" to be told "Yes. The message is for everyone who wants to live!" The illogicality of bracketing Protestants with non-Christians may have escaped the American Roman Catholic author, although roughly seventy-seven per cent of the U.S.A.'s population are non-Catholic and about ninety per cent in Great Britain, to say nothing of other parts of the globe. In terms of *unity* there seems to be still some way to go.

But there is perhaps little doubt that the ultimate unity of all Christians if not of all humanity, with the possible consequence of peace on earth, may be said to sum up the Medjugorje messages, and that peace is the means to that end. This was emphasized by the huge shining letters MIR (in the Serbo-Croat language PEACE) which appeared in the night sky over Medjugorje in August 1981, discussed on pages 45–46, and for which no natural explanation has ever been forthcoming.

As Mary's daily appearances and messages progressed it became clear that she was unfolding, through the Six, a perfectly clear and straightforward plan for the attainment of this peace, a plan which included five great themes – of Conversion, Prayer, Fasting, Penance and Faith. These themes persist, their function being to echo and illuminate the Gospel and to practise and apply its truth and teaching in daily life. This is the Gospel of Peace which Christ effectually brought to humanity by the cooperation of Mary his

Mother, who said in June 1983 to Jelena, of whom more anon:

> I have come to tell the world that God is truth; he exists. True happiness and the fulness of life are in him.

The personal peace which flows from the acceptance, understanding and practical realization of the five themes is probably the purpose, and certainly the reward, of knowledge of and pilgrimage to Medjugorje, the key being love – a love which implies the effort at least to try to observe Christ's two great commandments of love for God and neighbour.

In defining neighbourly love to the Croat Catholics to whom she appears and speaks, Mary said:

> Love your Moslem brothers. Love your Serbian brothers. Love those who govern you

words which echo Christ's words in chapter 15:17 of St John's Gospel[1] and bear very clearly on the history of Yugoslavia and her condition, perhaps particularly on what was happening there in 1991, when she was in a state of potential civil war. This state was brought about by the mutual distrust and lack of love which still existed between Serb and Croat, and the Croats-turned-Moslem who had succumbed to the Turks in the fifteenth century (pages 115–118), those who governed them being the Communist Party.

1 ''What I command you is to love one another''.

It has been said that to read the messages superficially is to fail to understand them, or even to dismiss them as banal and repetitive; but this could be to miss the point and to demonstrate the truth of Mark 6:52 in the context of miracles: "their minds were closed".

As a mother trains her children, so these messages can be absorbed and remembered:

Be aware that I am your Mother and that I have come on earth to teach you how to listen to God with love, how to pray with love.

Robert Llewelyn, an authority on the *Revelations of Divine Love* of the fourteenth century Julian of Norwich, observes that Christ said: "know that I am with you always; yes to the end of time";[2] but that if Mary had said: "I am always close to you" it would be considered banal, and equally so in her many references to peace, although Christ had said: "Peace be with you."[3]

After 1 March 1984 Mary's words in greeting the children were changed from the local "Praised be Jesus" of page 178 to "Dear Children" on her arrival each day and before her message for them, with "Thank you for having responded to my call" on her departure: awe-inspiring enough in the context of what was and is believed to be happening.

After the excitement of the first week of 24 June 1981,

2 Matthew 28:20.
3 John 20:19.

the messages to the children took the form of conversations with the Virgin, giving them confidence and answering the many questions they brought to her, both from themselves and others. But most of all, and with inexhaustible maternal love and patience, she taught them how to pray and of the value and importance of the five themes on the path of peace and in the search for God. Reaching Medjugorje for two days in June 1983, ''Mr Pentecost'' (pages 33–34) found that ''The whole place is charged with the love of God''; and when he asked some youngsters there why they were reading the Bible, he was told it was because the Blessed Mother had asked them to, in order to find out ''what Jesus will do for us and what he wants us to do for him'' echoing, perhaps unconsciously, the story of the water turned into wine, when Mary had said (of Christ), ''Do whatever he tells you.''[4]

It was on Thursday 1 March 1984 that the regular weekly messages began. Thursdays were chosen for several reasons, but chiefly perhaps because it was the day on which the Eucharist was instituted at the Last Supper; when Christ washed his disciples' feet as an example of love and service, afterwards saying: ''I give you a new commandment: love one another'', as recorded in St John's Gospel chapter 13. Two other reasons for the choice of Thursdays were a Eucharistic Congress at the Shrine of Maria Bistrica, due to take place that September, preparations for which included Thursday Eucharists as part of the celebrations to

4 John 2 1:11.

honour 300 years of the shrine's existence; and the people's preference for a mid-week day, when there were likely to be fewer foreign visitors. It was also the beginning of Lent in 1984.

The Thursday messages were thus the response of the people to Mary's request for them to come to church for a weekday Mass.

It was the visionary Marija to whom Mary invariably gave these messages, with the initial explanation to her on 1 March of

> I have especially chosen this parish and wish to lead it. I am watching over the parish with love . . .Every Thursday I will give you a special message.

Assuming Marija to be telling the truth, it has to be remembered that she and the other five can only receive and transmit what they hear according to their own capacity, much of what they hear being beyond their theological or even grammatical (pages 71–72) grasp; and as Father George Tutto points out in his *Medjugorje: Our Lady's Parish*, there is a great need for expert help in examining the messages critically, taking into account the human condition, imperfections and limitations of the visionaries. There is also the recurring problem of the necessarily rapid translation and distribution of the messages, in many languages and to many places, their initial purpose being generally regarded as publication.

Concurrently with the messages, the Six are being given the secrets, with only Mirjana and Ivanka having, by 1991, received the promised total of ten.

In her message of Thursday 9 June 1984 Mary said:

Tomorrow night pray for the Spirit of Truth, especially you from the parish. The Spirit of Truth is necessary for you in order to convey the messages just as I give them to you, not adding anything or taking anything away. . .I as your Mother say that you pray little.

17
One Family

Thursdays began as the result of a message to Jelena in February 1984, when Mary said that she would like the whole parish of Medjugorje to meet in the church for a special message once a week, so that she could guide them towards faith. The Thursday evening messages ended on 8 January 1987, when the Virgin thanked the parish through Marija for their response, cooperation and prayers, saying that what the Lord wanted had been accomplished and that she would continue to give them messages, but on the 25th of each month; and that she would remain with them to guide them.

The parish had by then been converted, and through them many others who had come to Medjugorje. Now Mary was calling them all to prayer with the heart, and on 25 May 1987:

I call on each one of you to decide for God and against Satan. . .I want each one of you to be happy here on earth and to be with me in heaven. That is, dear Children, the purpose of my coming here . . .

The 25th was the day of the month in June 1981 on which Mary first spoke to the Six. Jelena (Helena) was not one of them, but in December 1982, when only ten years old, she received what Laurentin calls the gift of interior light.

At school one day in the classroom the puzzle of a voice she could not identify was solved a week later, when she was sure of both seeing and hearing her guardian angel, who asked her not to be afraid and to fast and pray. She told Father Tomislav of this, and that she was happy, describing the angel as a child of about seven. In prayer a week later she asked this angel if she could see the *Gospa*, whereupon Mary appeared to her dressed in white and gold with stars round her head.

For those who find difficulty in taking this story seriously, it can be said that the appearances of saints of angels as heralds of the Mother of God have been recorded since at least the sixteenth century; by the Spanish St Teresa of Avila; the eighteenth century Russian St Seraphim of Sarov; and in the nineteenth and twentieth centuries by the Curé d'Ars and Catherine Labouré in France, the parish priest of Knock in Ireland, and three children at Fatima in Portugal, besides a Japanese nun in 1973 and a Nicaraguan layman in 1980.[1] It seems inconceivable that a perfectly normal child of ten, brought up in an obscure village, could have either heard or read of any of these accounts; and her youth, innocence, intelligence and calm temperament may have

1 See author's *Mother of Nations* (bibliography).

qualified her for the task she is believed to have been given.

Her visions and voices sound not unlike those of St Teresa of Avila, who wrote that she saw Christ and Mary with the "eyes of the soul" and was "sometimes addressed by interior voices". Unlike the Six, Jelena could neither touch Mary, see her three-dimensionally nor hear her audibly. The vision comes to her as a film seen with the eyes closed, the voice being the same interior locution experienced by, for example, Wayne Weible (page 37), Mirjana after she was given the tenth secret (page 77), and Ivan when he prayed during his military service (page 84). Jelena told Slavko that she only hears Mary when she is concentrating in prayer, and only sees her when she has been praying for at least fifteen minutes, which may have implications for others who pray.

Mary first came to Jelena on 29 December 1982, and in the following March to Jelena's friend and distant cousin Marijana with the same gifts of inner sight and hearing, Jelena being the elder by five months and the leader, and each substantiating the gifts of the other. Both girls were born in 1972.

When she began to hear Mary, Jelena asked if she might know the ten secrets, a rather touching and reassuringly human request from a small girl. But the Mother of God asked her forgiveness, telling her that she would be guided to God by another path and with different gifts.

Jelena's task was to respond to Mary's request of May 1983 to begin a prayer group of people, preferably young and without family commitments, who chose to be led and guided by her from words she would convey through Jelena; and that a priest should be a member of this group. Then aged eleven, Jelena turned to Father Tomislav Vlasic who advised the Six spiritually, and he became its chaplain. Mary told her that one month would be given to form the group, who must be willing to put themselves in God's hands and to pray for at least three hours a day – time which could be spent in the church (where time goes surprisingly fast) but must include half an hour every morning and evening – and that they should meet at least once a week. They were further asked to put off for four years any decision as to a career, marriage or vocation. Mary asked that meanwhile they would fear nothing, particularly interference from Satan, that they would fast twice a week on bread and water, and that they would trust in God while she guided them in prayer and life.

The group was initially composed of over fifty young people of both sexes, and included Marija as the only representative of the Six; and as well as this large group, a small group led by the Virgin through Jelena from August 1984 say that they see and hear Christ as well as his Mother.

Jelena attributed to Satan what she described as a terrible voice heard when saying the Lord's Prayer, a voice telling her to stop it and not to listen to Mary. The Virgin speaks to the groups through these two young girls, who hear her unsought as they hear the voice of conscience, usually speaking to them almost daily during the service of Holy Communion when they experience great peace and inner joy.

They pray aloud spontaneously, or meditate in silence, or recite the rosary; at home, on Krizevac, or in the church. They are encouraged by the Virgin, who tells them that if they give their time to God they will be able to do all that is required of them, besides growing in spiritual awareness and being enabled to make right choices; and that every agitation and disorder come from Satan.

From these groups many more sprang up in Medjugorje, meeting on several evenings each week and affecting not only the visionaries and the parish, but also the pilgrims and through them, in diverse, gradual but unerring ways, the world.

Mary offered a pattern and guidance for prayer in her first Thursday message of March 1984, when Marija heard that Medjugorje was the chosen parish, (page 185) and then in July:

Dear Children, I ask you to read the Bible in your homes every day.

Always pray before your work and end your work with a prayer . . .God will bless you and your work . . .In prayer you will find rest.

A request through Jelena was that every Thursday, in the church if possible, but otherwise with their families, the people should read and meditate upon the passage of St Matthew's Gospel chapter 6 verses 24-34 which suggests making certain decisions: essentially to serve God not money; to trust in God; to have no worry about our life or tomorrow; and that God knows our needs and will look after each one, with the useful counsel in April of the same year that it is necessary to persevere in prayer, and to ''read the Gospel and you will understand everything'' *before* starting to pray.

Mary's advice on a way of meditation, again through Jelena in 1984 was:

> I will give you a spiritual secret so that you can be protected from evil and always united with God. Pray in the morning and read a passage from the Gospel. Impress it on your mind and in your heart and carry it with you through the day. In moments of crisis meditate on it again. If your faith is strong Satan cannot harm you.

In terms of listening to God, the likely action of the Holy Spirit in prayer may be deduced from a recorded conversation in 1985 between Slavko and Jelena, during which she told him that she had noticed days on which the subject of the priest's homily or sermon in the church repeated a message given to her by Mary the day before.

Ivan's prayer group, described on pages 84 and 87, has remained steadfast in meeting on one or other of the hills on two if not three evenings a week, and is unique not only because it is led by Mary but also because she herself then appears to Ivan and any other of the Six who may be present – mostly Marija and Vicka – staying with them longer than at the 6.40 appearance each evening. It was Marija who held the group together during Ivan's conscription; and although others who are present may be aware of diffuse light or a strong sense of her presence, none but the Six can see Mary.

Rosehip Hill, which became Krizevac or Hill of the Cross in 1933 (page 42), has drawn people to it in prayer from that date, as it drew Ivan and his prayer group in 1982 and still draws pilgrims of all ages, who climb the steep and stony track as a challenge, with awe, in penitence, with thanksgiving, or for all these and other reasons.

Those who accept that the Virgin has been permitted by God to come to Medjugorje, as the place of her last earthly visits,[2] also accept her message of 30 August 1984:

the cross was in God's plan when you built it

a plan that may be said to be still unfolding.

''I have especially chosen this parish'', said Mary (page 185): a scenically beautiful parish round whose church in early 1981 lived a farming community of five villages. Their inhabitants had long been engaged in territorial feuds and family quarrels, for which reason the church had a capacity of 600 and was sited in a field on neutral ground. Its construction was begun in 1937, four years after Krizevac, but war and Communism delayed its completion until 1969, when it replaced a smaller church nearby which had been damaged by an earth-tremor, and three outlying chapels including that at Surmanci. But the new church

2 See p. 96.

was seldom full until late 1981, when an extraordinary transformation took place in the five surrounding villages.

Families ceased to quarrel, they elected to spend time daily in their church, and they were glad to offer constant hospitality to the waves of pilgrims, foreign or otherwise, who poured continually on to their quiet shores. As each wave receded another took its place, and so the rhythm has been repeated year in year out, as God is sought and found in Medjugorje.

Is this the parish chosen by God to become, despite human error and encroaching materialism, a pattern for all parishes? A place where a pilgrim with no knowledge of the language may go quietly home to an unfailing welcome by a village family, finding that on the walk back from Podbrdo a smile and a hand raised in salute is returned in a spirit of brother-or sisterhood from the fields, the roads and the open doors: and that a man in a Franciscan friar's habit is welcomed with hugs and laughter as he goes on his way?

It is the same remote parish whose families, despite feuds, have always prayed together, whose houses have always been blessed with holy water and whose ancient prayer round yule logs on Christmas Eve, besides being the normal greeting (page 178), has always been ''Praised be Jesus and Mary'': to which Mary said she had come because there were many believers there; and whose people, from late 1981, have welcomed all comers however demanding, because through the Six they believed that the Mother of God had asked them to open their homes and hearts, and to welcome the pilgrims as if they were their own family.

These are the same people who are no longer addicted to alcohol and blasphemy swearing, ''which the Croats have developed to a fine art of inventiveness'',[3] having been a spectre which haunted the Church in those parts; a skill they are thought to have inherited from their Bogomil ancestors (chapter 9), who believed that only the soul was created by God. The body and the material world were Satan's, and to escape the devil and his creations their ideals were to renounce possessions, marriage, meat, wine, churches and icons. The proof that they had accepted Christianity included indulgence in marriage and meat-eating, and the use by both sexes of blasphemous and obscene oaths which, with their tombstones, were the only Bogomil legacies in Medjugorje by 1981.

These are the same people whose young ones, instructed by the Virgin for four years, were found by Bob Faricy in 1986 to have reached an advanced stage of contemplative prayer, always conscious of the presence of God though behaving and dressing (in jeans) like anyone else; and whose community and family lives reflect the love and brother/sisterhood of the Christians of the Early Church.

It seems characteristic of Medjugorje that visitors feel immediately at home there, as do the Medjugorje pilgrims who may later meet by chance or design elsewhere.

3 Alexander p. 39 (bibliography).

The prayer groups instituted and instructed by the Virgin or vision have united as one family not only the people of this parish especially chosen by her, but also the many millions of people from all continents who share the experience of having prayed at or at least been to Medjugorje.

18
Revolution

Dragan Kozina, a man born in Medjugorje in 1956 and therefore aged 25 in 1981, considered the hullabaloo to be merely a joke or the effect of drugs; but when, after three days, he decided to join the crowd of a thousand or so people on the hill of Podbrdo to try to assess what was happening, he became aware of a supernatural presence so powerful that he claims that he *knew*, as a fact, that the story was true.

Marrying in 1980, he lived near his parents, content with a livelihood from selling grapes and tobacco when not employed in a government office in the neighbouring town of Citluk. But in 1983, as he saw increasing numbers of homeless visitors wandering about the village he began to build his present house, with his own hands and casual help from friends and his father, who was one of the many migrant labourers in Germany. He still cannot understand how the work got done in four years. His intention was to look after the Yugoslav and Italian pilgrims with no idea of making money, regarding them as fellow Christians rather than as tourists, and was surprised to find that his guests became international. Through a disagreement with the local Communist Party leaders he was handcuffed in May 1981, losing his job and narrowly avoiding imprisonment. Problems connected with his Christian allegiance did not, however, prevent him finding further employment in Citluk until, in 1987, he decided to work on pilgrim accommodation in Medjugorje.

He came to see that there was nothing wrong in making a living from this hospitality, but that there were two motives: to serve God by helping pilgrims, or to make money, and he chose to serve God. He and his wife enjoy meeting and providing shelter for the pilgrims, though they are not alone in feeling the lack of privacy that this entails. He has learned English, the language most spoken by visitors to Medjugorje; he finds no difficulty in getting to church every day, unlike certain other busy innkeepers; and he is making enough money to feed his five children. Like the visionary Marija's elder brother Andrea (page 88), once a sceptic and now another dedicated innkeeper, he says all the local families have in some way experienced the presence of the Virgin Mary since June 1981.

His story is typical of the lives of many others in Medjugorje, illustrating the practical effects of a biblical meditation advised by the *Gospa* (page 191). He puts God before money and is at peace; and though he may wonder what will become of his three-story house if pilgrimage should cease, his trust in God sustained him during the work of building for pilgrims who might never appear.

But still they come, providing rich pickings for

innkeepers whose God may have become money, among whom are some who had abandoned Christianity but who returned to it after the collapse of the Communist government in 1990.

What is regarded as a continuing miracle is the atmosphere of peace and love which pervades the church, and the orderliness of the continual throng of people who move quietly about the hillsides, lanes and cafes; crowds who neither require nor receive control or coordination, are non-political, and among whom there are people who have prayed for the first time in their lives. This too is a continuing miracle for the priests from almost all nations who hear confessions there.

Mary's essential message, always patiently repeated, is to believe in the existence of God; to decide for God and against Satan (page 187); and to accept Christ's words of 'Doubt no longer but believe', spoken after his resurrection to doubting Thomas and before he said: ''Happy are those who have not seen and yet believe.''[1] These were words echoed by Mary on day five, when the children asked why she did not appear to everyone in the church. When, on day three, they asked her why she came, they were told that she wished to be with them

to convert and reconcile the whole world

and thus bring peace to the visionaries, the parish and humanity.

Two of the people who have found peace in Medjugorje are Bernard Ellis and Anka Blasevic.

1 John 20:28–9.

Bernard is an Englishman educated as an orthodox Jew, who has for thirty years been the owner/manager of a successful company which sells steel to Third World countries. As a boy, he had thought of becoming a rabbi. In 1983 his Roman Catholic wife suggested a visit to Medjugorje and to please her he agreed, thinking that at least it would be a holiday near the Adriatic resort of Dubrovnik. But his trip to Medjugorje was the first of over twenty, and he is now a Christian.

He had regarded Christ not as the Son of God but as the prophet of Christians, and Mary the Mother of God as a charming fairy-tale but one that was intellectually unacceptable, though aware that Mary had been a Jewess. Moved by the hospitality, love, friendship and peace which he found at Medjugorje, he considers his conversion to Christianity to have been the immediate answer to a prayer, in which he was supported by Father Jozo, that the Holy Spirit would reveal to him the truth of the Gospel of Peace. Both he and his wife see his conversion as symbolizing the fulfilment of Old Testament prophecy – for example Isaiah chapter 53 – and they are now active in supporting Medjugorje financially, by their prayers and in many other ways.

Anka is a Croat educated by Communists, who grew up with a contempt for Christianity. Having spent a year in Mexico preparing her degree thesis she went to a meditation centre in Italy, still an atheist, to search for her life's purpose. She then thought of going to a monastery in Holland, but instead acted on a hunch to return to Dubrovnik and work as a tourist guide. She speaks fluent English.

Her first assignment was to interpret for a group of pilgrims to Medjugorje, in preparation for which she decided to go there ahead of the group. She looked inside the church during a celebration of the Eucharist, but had no idea of what was going on; she noticed with interest, however, that when the people left the altar to return to their places, having been given something to eat, they seemed to radiate a light which shone towards her.

Like Bernard, she was helped by Father Jozo and is now a Christian, her work being chiefly the translation of Jozo's talks to English-speaking pilgrims.

It may be remembered that the Virgin appeared to Pasa Djano (page 31), telling Mirjana that the piety of this Moslem woman was a model for everyone, and that Pasa was a true believer. This may have some relevance to the account of an Anglican priest, who wrote: ''At an international Christian congress in the Phillipines in 1989, it was reported that Moslems in different parts of the world have recently seen visions of Jesus appearing to them – evidently unsought and without human intermediary.'' It is not as yet clear whether these visionaries identified Jesus as God incarnate or as the child who said from his cradle: ''I am the servant of Allah. He has given me the Gospel and ordained me a prophet;'' the child of whom the Lord's messenger (the Angel Gabriel) told Mary the Virgin: ''He shall be a sign to mankind.''[2]

The words ''Love your Moslem brothers. Love your Serbian brothers'' (page 182) are also illustrated by a

2 Koran pp. 33–34.

Serbian Orthodox woman who had spent ten days in Medjugorje, and on Slavko's enquiry of ''How are you?'' told him that she was well, because in Medjugorje she had found the people of God.

There seems little doubt that privately, and certainly in the Medjugorje region, Serb and Croat get along very well together. The quarrel is political only, their ancient enmity (page 120) being deliberately perpetuated by the Communist government of Serbia. Forty-five years of Communist rule in Slovenia, Croatia and Bosnia-Hercegovina ended with free elections in May 1990.[3]

An appeal from the Patriarch of the Serbian Orthodox Church that Christmas should be made a public holiday was rejected by the President of the Republic of Serbia in January 1991, causing the Patriarch to protest that Christmas was at that time a public holiday not only in Slovenia and Croatia, but also in the USSR.[4]

In December 1990 evidence of peace, love and healing appeared in Surmanci. The inconspicuous path of page 132 had been replaced by a road of granite chips leading straight to the concrete column, from the top of which flew the flag of Serbia with a small black flag of mourning. That pit of anguished death has been sanctified by a stone cross cemented to the concrete surface, and by a wooden cross secured to a nearby tree, symbols of the reconciliation – the peace, forgiveness and love – for which the weeping

3 *The Times* of 11 and 21 February 1991.
4 Keston News Service No. 368.

Madonna pleaded to Marija (page 25) on 26 June 1981.

The present concrete surface dates only from the end of Communist rule, when it was possible for Serbs to excavate the seventy-five metre deep crater it covers, and remove from it the three metres of human bones it contained: the remains of almost a thousand old men, women and children. Among those who looked on, a bent old man told Gabriel Meyer[5] that now he could die, since his wife and six children – the youngest aged five months – had died in that pit.

Very early on 24 November 1990 twenty-five trucks draped in black took the dead through Medjugorje for their Christian burial in Prebilovci, the village near the Neretva River from which they had been rounded up on that August day of 1941.

If there were Franciscan priests among the Ustase perpetrators of this atrocity – the heavy burden borne by Slavko and his brethren (page 146) – a Vatican Directive to (Franciscan) clergy in the Independent State of Croatia dated 24 July 1941 is relevant. It states that any Franciscan is banned from being a member of the Croatian Ustasa movement; and that Franciscans must not take any part in the persecution of Serbs and Jews. The Directive was published in full on 24 February 1989 in *Glas Koncila*, the Yugoslav Roman Catholic fortnightly news tabloid.

In the light of these events at Surmanci on Mount Crnica, and given that the purported apparitions of 1981 and thereafter did in fact occur, it is difficult to accept as coincidental the choice of Podbrdo hill on

5 USA *National Catholic Register*, January 1991.

the same mountain of Crnica as the site of the first visions; perhaps Mary's plea of "Peace, Peace, Peace. Be reconciled" becomes the more significant. Marija, to whom alone the Virgin's call was given (page 25) could not then have known of the sanctification of the pit of Surmanci, even had she known of its existence.

It seems that all happiness will follow a response to this paramount call for peace, but a revolution may have to come first: the choice of a radical turn from whatever may be keeping us from God, be it hatred, envy, drink, drugs, immorality or merely money and the priorities which go with its lack or possession.

It looks as if Medjugorje points to hope in youth. This was the understanding of Ernest Williams, a graduate employee of British Aerospace (born 1962) who went to Medjugorje first in 1987; and observing the huge crowds of young people it attracted, he was inspired to initiate what has become an International Festival of Youth.

Since 1989 Youth 2000 has brought the young of twenty-four countries to Medjugorje each July-August for a week of praise, prayer and healing. In 1990, when six thousand young people were present, there was strong support from those countries of Eastern Europe then very recently liberated from Communist government. In 1991 the politically necessary cancellation of the event may be a merely temporary set-back.

REMEMBER

19
St Bernard

In May and June 1982 Mary told the Six that she had come to call the world to conversion for the last time, and that in Medjugorje her appearances are the last in the world.

Although there have undoubtedly been many false reports of visions of the Blessed Virgin Mary and there will almost certainly be many more, there are good grounds for believing that she has been seen, if not heard, in all continents and for many centuries. The reasons for her appearances are always the same: to present God to the world anew, to remind humanity of the Gospel of Christ, and to show her maternal concern by warning of the likely and unhappy consequences of ignoring her increasingly urgent message of conversion to belief and of turning back to God while there is still time.

A prayer which has been in use since the late fifteenth century, and whose origin is thus pre-Reformation, is popularly supposed to have been written by St Bernard of Clairvaux (who died in 1153), probably because he wrote of Mary in terms which evoke this prayer; but its author is unknown. It is called the Memorare, or Remember, and its relevance here is that in 1842 it was the means of converting an intelligent and particularly sceptical unbeliever to almost instant faith through a vision of Mary, of whom he told ''eight honest and trustworthy men'' who corroborated his stable state of mind: ''I have seen her as I see you.'' The man was Alphonse Ratisbonne, whose story is told in *Mother of Nations, Visions of Mary.*[1]

Mary is honoured because she was chosen to become the Mother of God; because she is the holiest of all saints; and because she became the Mother of humankind from the time of Christ's last words to St John: ''This is your Mother.''[2] It is for these reasons that she is asked to intercede in heaven. Here is the prayer:

Remember, O most loving Virgin Mary, that never was it known that anyone who fled to your protection, implored your help, or sought your intercession was left unaided. Inspired by this confidence, we fly unto you, O Virgin of Virgins, our Mother. To you we come, before you we stand, sinful and sorrowful. O Mother of the Word incarnate, despise not our petitions, but in your mercy hear and answer me.

These words may be said to epitomize the relationship of the Six with Mary. They look to her

1 Ashton (bibliography).
2 John 19:27.

as their heavenly Mother; they listen to her, knowing
that she loves them and will listen to their prayers and
help them; she asks them to pray and to encourage
others to do so; and they understand her when she
quotes Christ's words to St Thomas: ''Happy are those
who have not seen and yet believe.''

They look forward with intense happiness to her
presence and dread the prospect of her eventual
absence; but when asked if they had to choose between
continuing to see her or being present at Holy
Communion, they are in no doubt: they would choose
Holy Communion, knowing that then Christ always
comes to them and that Mary's sole purpose in being
visible is to bring them to Christ, and through them
to bring the world back to God.

To what extent they may have arrived at this truth
themselves, or how much of it they may have learned
through priestly counsel, can only be conjectured at
this stage.

EPILOGUE

It has been suggested that in the case of Medjugorje the essential function of Devil's Advocate (page 61) for critical examination of the alleged miracle is ably fulfilled by Bishop Zanic of Mostar.

In July 1981 the bishop let it be known that he was profoundly convinced that the children were speaking the truth, and in August of that year his letter to the same effect was published in *Glas Koncila*, the Yugoslav Croat Catholic newspaper; yet he later denounced the Six as liars, said that Tomislav Vlasic had invented the whole story, and in October 1984 he informed the world press that the visions were false.

This information was conveyed in his lengthy letter "The Present Position", which prompted Archbishop Franic of Split to write to Cardinal Ratzinger in Rome (chapter 4) begging him to appoint an International Commission of Inquiry and saying: "The twenty-three page letter of the Bishop of Mostar, which contains grave calumnies against the friars, against Father Laurentin and the visionaries, has already caused scandal . . ."

The bishop, however, was not to be silenced. On 18
January 1990 he issued a further pamphlet, in which
he not only reiterated his earlier calumnies but added
several more. This drew a stern response from the
Franciscan theologian Father Ljudevit Rupcic in a book
entitled *The Truth about Medjugorje.*

With documentary and other evidence, Rupcic notes
that by his early support of the visions, expressed both
orally and in a letter of September 1981 to the Yugoslav
President, the bishop was suspected of encouraging
insurrection against the Communist government. He
was therefore summoned to Sarajevo in August 1981
and threatened by the Secret Police (UDBA) with
imprisonment if he did not immediately discourage the
visionaries and put a stop to the increasing pilgrimage,
which involved the assembly of huge crowds.

The bishop's reaction to this threat was to avoid
Medjugorje and adopt a policy of temporary silence
on the subject. Exposed to the same threat at the same
time, Father Jozo was arrested and sentenced on 17
August 1981 to three and a half years hard labour,
commuted to eighteen months.

After his release on 18 February 1983 Jozo called on
the bishop, who told him that he had been under
pressure from his secular priests, who were against
supporting the Franciscans in Medjugorje; and that he
could not have gone to prison for Medjugorje, nor did
he wish "to go from being a bishop to assistant pastor
of a village". But if the bishop was not inspired to
martyrdom for his belief, it is perhaps fair to remember
that the strength of Jozo's conviction lay in his private
revelation of 2 July 1981 (pages 27–28).

Perhaps the enigma of the bishop's early change of heart, only partially explained by the Hercegovina Case, is at last made plain. It also becomes clear that his evidence can hardly be regarded as reliable, and that his campaign of apparent defamation and deliberate misrepresentation has two aims: to persuade the Vatican against authentication of the visions, and to bring about the abolition of the local Franciscan Province.

The Commission of The Yugoslav Bishops' Conference appointed in January 1987 (page 60) issued a communique, thought to be so diplomatic as to be contradictory, on its special session at Zagreb from 27-8 November 1990. The communique stated in effect that up to the present time the bishops cannot affirm that they are dealing with supernatural apparitions or revelation, but that they are disposed to help the resident bishop (i.e. Zanic) in organizing the pastoral work of Medjugorje.

Publication of this text had not been authorized either by the Yugoslav bishops or the Vatican, but it was leaked to a Catholic news agency by Bishop Zanic, with the no doubt anticipated consequence that ''t sounded a clear note of caution to Catholics''.

Laurentin commented in January 1991 that it would have been impossible for the Yugoslav bishops to have been more positive, since the visions are alleged to continue and the disclosure of the secrets is still awaited. In February Cardinal Ratzinger observed that there was no proof yet of supernatural occurrences in Medjugorje, while Archbishop Franic considered any ambiguity in the statement was accounted for by the bishops' concern not to offend their colleague of Mostar. But an auxiliary bishop of Rome who sees the Pope frequently, the Czechoslovakian Monsignor Paul Hnilica S.J., points out that the Roman Catholic Church's continuing silence concerning Medjugorje implies approval; and he quotes John Paul II as having said: "If I wasn't a Pope I'd be in Medjugorje already!"

It is clear that the official investigating committee had not been dissolved and continued to review evidence about the visions after July 1991; and that, as Slavko said in September 1990 (page 157), the (Catholic) pilgrims no longer seem interested in the authentication of the events by a Bishop's Commission. The presence of God in Medjugorje is unmistakable, even to most sceptics.

At the end of August 1981, a few weeks after the great sign of MIR (peace) appeared in the night sky, Mary said: "I am the Queen of Peace", and in the following January she told the Six that the call to peace is also addressed to the bishop.

In January and February 1991 her messages included encouragement to grasp the rosary, and to make peace rather than to speak of it. "The saying of the rosary unites the soul to God," says Robert Llewelyn in *A Doorway to Silence* (see bibliography); and that "in saying the rosary you submit yourself to the prayers of Mary and, by implication, to the prayers of the whole company of heaven. On every bead this submission is renewed." Another Anglican, Archbishop George Carey, spoke at Walsingham in 1988 of his discovery that he would not be obscuring

Christ if he prayed with and to the saints, and to Christ's Mother as well.

The rosary as an aid to meditation on the fifteen main events of the Gospel of Peace – the joyful, sorrowful and glorious mysteries – is an essential part of the prayer of the heart, to which Mary constantly invites the Six; a far deeper prayer than mere routine or recitation, and one that may lead to the gift of contemplation defined by Michael Ramsey as ''a liberation from out restless brain-activity into the depth of the love of God in our souls''.[1]

It may be asked if all this is a fanciful tale of invention, about which certain Roman Catholics among others have tended to become euphoric; happening in a delightfully remote and scenically lovely village to a few captivatingly simple youngsters in what was a Communist country; a country which has grasped the financial advantages of handling what looks like becoming permanent Christian pilgrimage? Or is it, on the contrary, something of potentially universal and shattering significance?

Perhaps for the present Medjugorje may be summed up in the words attributed to Dominique Peyramale, the Dean of Lourdes at the time of Bernadette's visions in 1858:

For those who believe no explanation is necessary. For those who do not believe, no explanation is possible.

1 Mother Mary Clare, S.L.G. (see bibliography).

APPENDICES

Chronology

August	The Virgin says "I am the Queen of Peace".	216
August 6	MIR (Peace) seen in huge letters of light against the night sky.	45
August 17	Father Jozo is arrested and imprisoned.	28
December	Father Tomislav Vlasic becomes spiritual director to the Six.	56
1982 January	Visions take place in room to right of church altar, until March 1985. It is since known as the Chapel of the Apparitions.	
January	Father Slavko arrived in Medjugorje.	14
June	Satan appeared to Mirjana.	76
December	The Virgin speaks to Jelena for the first time.	188.
December 25	The Virgin gives Mirjana the tenth secret, and no longer appears to her daily, but annually on her birthday, 18 March.	75
1983 February 18	Father Jozo is released from prison, but is forbidden by the bishop to return to Medjugorje.	214
May	The Virgin asks Jelena to form a prayer group.	189
November 30	Through Marija, the Virgin asked that Father Tomislav should write of Medjugorje to the bishop and the Pope.	
December 2	Father Torrislav did so.	
1984 March 1	The Virgin, through Marija, begins to give the Thursday messages, ending in January 1987.	86, 184
August 30	The Virgin tells the Six (for the parish) that Krizevac was in God's plan when they built it.	193
October 30	The bishop circulates a long letter on "The Present Position" to the effect that in his view the visions are false.	57, 214

1985 April	The bishop forbids the use of room to right of altar for the Six each evening. Instead, the visions take place in the rectory each evening.	140
May 6	The Virgin gives Ivanka the tenth secret and promises to come to her every year on 25 June.	73
June 27	Father Peter Ljubicic is chosen by Mirjana to publish the secrets when the Virgin tells her.	77
September	Father Slavko replaces Tomislav as spiritual director to the Six.	140
1986 December 28	Ivanka married to Raiko Elez.	74
June	Ivan begins a year of compulsory military service.	
1987 January 25	The Virgin gives through Marija the first of the messages received on the 25th of every month, replacing the Thursday messages.	87
July 25	At a Medjugorje confirmation service the bishop preaches his ''hell sermon''.	60
September 9	The bishop forbids the use of rectory for visionaries. The visions take place in the choir loft.	
November 11	Daughter born to Ivanka.	75
1988 October 6	Father Slavko becomes Vice-Master of Novices at Humac, but continues as spiritual director to the Six.	
December 16	Marija undergoes kidney donor operation.	88
1989 July	Inauguration of annual International Youth Prayer Gathering in Medjugorje as Youth 2000.	204
September 16	Mirjana married to Marco Soldo.	77
1990 May	Free elections end Communist rule in Croatia, Slovenia and Bosnia-Hercegovina.	202

Bibliography

Alexander, Stella, *Church and State in Yugoslavia since 1945*. Cambridge University Press 1979

Allbright, Judith, *Our Lady of Medjugorje*. Riehle Foundation 1988

Allison Peers, E., *Mother of Carmel*. S.C.M. 1979

Ashton, Joan, *Mother of Nations*. Marshall Pickering 1988

Barberic, Slavko, *Pray with the Heart*. Parish, Viganj 1988

Basler, Duro, *The Shrine of Our Lady, Siroki Brieg*. Franciscan, Zagreb 1984

Batty, Peter, Ed., *MIR Recorder*. St Leonards, Sussex 1985-8

Beeson, Trevor, *Discretion and Valour*. Collins Fount 1982

Bena, Angelo, *The Events of Medjugorje*. Velar, Italy 1988

Bubalo/Girard, *Mary Queen of Peace Stay with Us*. Montreal 1988

Bubalo, Janko, *A Thousand Encounters with the Blessed Virgin Mary of Medjugorje*. Chicago 1987

Carey, Archbishop George, *Walsingham Review for Christmas 1990*

Citluk and Brotnjo Tourist Guidebook 1987, MOSTAR Tourist Guidebook. Zagreb 1985

Connell, Jan, *Queen of the Cosmos*. Paraclete Press, U.S.A. 1990

Craig, Mary, *Spark from Heaven*. Hodder & Stoughton 1988

Cross and Livingstone, *Oxford Dictionary of the Christian Church*. Oxford University Press 1985

Faricy, Robert and Rooney, Lucy, *Mary Queen of Peace*. Veritas, Dublin 1984

Faricy, Robert and Rooney, Lucy, *Medjugorje Unfolds*. Fowler Wright 1985

Faricy, Robert and Rooney, Lucy, *Medjugorje Journal*. McGrimmons 1987

Faricy, Robert and Rooney, Lucy, *A Medjugorje Retreat*. Fowler Wright 1989

Foley, Richard, Ed., *Medjugorje Messenger*. Medjugorje Centre 1986-91

Gitty, Serena, *Sunday Times Magazine*. London 1985

Gobbi, Stefano, *Our Lady Speaks to Her Beloved Priests*. Marian Movement of Priests, New South Wales 1973 reprint 1990

Good News, bi-monthly periodical of Charismatic Renewal

Grant, Bob, *New Wine, New Wine Skins*. Grant Books, Worcs. 1988

Hickey, Tony, Ed., *MIR, Manchester*. Prestwich 1985-91

Hocken, Peter, *One Lord, One Spirit, One Body*. Paternoster Press, Exeter 1987

Israel, Martin, *The Dark Face of Reality*. Collins Fount 1989

Johnston, Francis, *Fatima: The Great Sign*. Augustine Pub. 1984

Jones, Michael E., *Medjugorje: The Untold Story*. Fidelity Press, U.S.A. 1989

Keston College News Service (fortnightly publication)

Koran, The (translated N.J. Dawood). Penguin 1976

Kraljevic, Svetozar, *The Apparitions of Our Lady at Medjugorje*. Franciscan Chicago 1984

Laurentin, René and Rupcic, Ljudevit, *Is the Virgin Mary Appearing in Medjugorje?* Word Among Us, U.S.A. 1984

Laurentin, René, *The Apparitions of Medjugorje Prolonged*. Riehle, U.S.A. 1986

Laurentin, René, *Latest News of Medjugorje*. Riehle, U.S.A. 1987

Laurentin, René, *Seven Years of Apparitions*. Riehle, U.S.A. 1988

Laurentin, René, *Report on Apparitions*. Riehle, U.S.A. 1989

Laurentin, René, *Eight Years*. Riehle, U.S.A. 1989

Laurentin, René, *The Apparitions of the Blessed Virgin Mary Today*. Veritas Dublin 1988

Laurentin, René, *Bernadette of Lourdes*. Darton, Longman 1979

Laurentin, René and Lejeune, René, *Messages and Teachings of Mary at Medjugorje*. Riehle, U.S.A. 1988

Laurentin, René & Joyeux, Henri, *Scientific & Medical Studies on the Apparitions at Medjugorje*. Veritas, Dublin 1987

Lawrence, Sir John, *The Hammer and The Cross*. B.B.C. London 1986

Llewelyn, Robert, *A Doorway to Silence*. Darton, Longman and Todd 1986

Luther, Martin, *The Magnificat Explained*. Michigan, U.S.A. reprinted 1982

Maindron, Gabriel, *Des Apparitions à Kibeho*. OEIL, Paris 1984

Marchi, John de, *Fatima from the Beginning*. Portugal 1983

Marin, Jakov, *Queen of Peace in Medjugorje*. Riehle, U.S.A. 1988

McKenna, Briege, *Miracles Do Happen*. Veritas, Dublin 1987

Mother Mary Clare, *Encountering the Depths*. Darton, Longman & Todd 1981

Neame, Alan, *The Happening at Lourdes*. Catholic Book Club 1968

O'Carroll, Michael, *Medjugorje: Facts, Documents, Theology*. Veritas, Dublin 1986

Parsons, Heather, *A Light Between the Hills*. Kildanore, Dublin 1989

Pelletier, Joseph A., *The Queen of Peace Visits Medjugorje*. Worcester, U.S.A. 1985

Pervan, Tomislav, *Queen of Peace*. Franciscan, U.S.A. 1986

Plunkett, Dudley, *Queen of Prophets*. Darton, Longman & Todd 1990

Riehle Foundation, Ed., *A Man Named Father Jozo*. Riehle. U.S.A. 1988

Rupcic, Ljudevit, *The Great Falsification*. Yugoslavia 1988

Rupcic, Ljudevit, *The Truth about Medjugorje*. Yugoslavia 1990

Sivric, Ivo, *The Hidden Side of Medjugorje*. Psilog, Canada 1988

Stacpoole, O.S.B., Alberic, Ed., *Mary and the Churches*. Columba Press 1987

Suenens, Léon Joseph, *A New Pentecost?* Collins Fount 1977

The Tablet: Christopher Cviic and others

The Times

Thurian, Max, *Mary Mother of the Lord, Figure of the Church*. Mowbray 1985

Tutto, George, *Mary Mother of God, Mother of Man*. Leicester 1984

Tutto, George, *Medjugorje: Our Lady's Parish*. St Leonards, Sussex 1985

Tutto, George, *Living the Gospel with Our Lady*. Manchester Medjugorje Centre 1991

Tutto, George, *Medjugorje: School of Prayer*. Enfield, Middlesex 1986

Vlasic, Tomislav, *Our Lady Queen of Peace*. St Leonards, Sussex 1983

Vlasic, Tomislav and Barberic, Slavko, *The Grey, Blue and Red Books of Meditations*. Milan 1985-6

Walsingham Review Christmas 1990

Ware, Timothy, *The Orthodox Church*. Penguin 1983

Weible, Wayne, *Medjugorje, the Message*. Paraclete Press U.S.A. 1989

Zanic, Pavao, *The Truth about Medjugorje*. Mostar, Yugoslavia 1990

Books specifically about Medjugorje may be obtained from Medjugorje Centres at 326 High Road, Ilford, Essex IG1 1QP and/or 5 Oaklands Drive, Prestwich, Manchester M25 5LJ.

Index